Functional Skills HANDBOOK for

ENGLISH Level 1

By Ann O'Toole & Marian Shepard

Highfield House
Heavens Walk
Lakeside
Doncaster
DN4 5HZ

Published by
Highfield.co.uk Limited 2012

ISBN 978-1-907751-82-0
1st Edition November 2012

0845 2260350
01302 363277
0845 2260360
highfield.co.uk

Functional Skills HANDBOOK for ENGLISH

contents

Introduction

This resource book has been written to help you understand all the different topics in English that you will need to know to pass a Functional Skills test at Level 1.

Each topic has been organised under its own heading so that you can easily find the pages you need to help you with anything you are not yet sure about, with suggestions for practice examples from everyday life.

Important facts, things to remember and areas where special care should be taken are highlighted throughout this book.

Marian Shepard

Marian, a registered subject expert in English for Ofqual, is an ex-head teacher who managed curriculum delivery through a school and specialised in English.
She has extensive experience in assessment of English at KS2 and KS3, including developing test materials for students and training for markers. Marian was the marking programme leader for KS2 English in 2007-9 and currently is writing comprehension and grammar items for Year 7 tests.

Marian is now applying her experience to assessment of English in the post compulsory sector and marks Level 1 Functional Skills English tests for Awarding Organisations.

➡ Introducing the Authors

Ann O'Toole

Ann has experience of managing and delivering English in FE, as a tutor; in ACL Colleges as the Head of Workforce Development; was Academic Manager for Literacy and Numeracy in Prison.

She has trained tutors using SFL core curricula and continues to advise on embedding FS into the delivery of apprenticeships.

In addition, Ann undertakes inspections of PFE and English Languages Schools, reporting on the quality of provision and the extent to which standards are met.

Marian Shepard and Ann O'Toole are independent education consultants, with extensive experience of delivering and managing the teaching and learning of English in a range of settings.

They are skilled in producing educational resources of the highest quality that ensure students engage with the learning process, are able to reach their potential and meet their learning goals.

Speaking, Listening and Communication

This section is about speaking, listening and communicating in formal and informal discussions. To achieve Level 1 you need to do the following:

- Make relevant and extended contributions to discussions, allowing for and responding to the input from others
- Prepare for and contribute to the formal discussion of ideas and opinions
- Make different kinds of contributions to discussions
- Present information/points of view clearly and in appropriate language

→ Developing Listening Skills

As part of your assessment and in real life, you will need to take part in discussions, allowing for the contributions of other participants and responding in an appropriate way. This means that you need to listen to what others are saying.

There is a big difference between hearing and listening.
Hearing is a physical ability.
Listening is a skill that can be learned and developed.

> **Key Point:**
>
> **Hearing** is a physical ability.
> **Listening** is a skill.

- If your family and friends say that you are a good listener, they are paying you a compliment.
- If you can listen, understand and remember what you have been told, you have a valuable skill.

5 steps of active listening...

Step 1:
Pay attention to what the speaker is telling you.

You should give the speaker your full **attention**.

You should **listen** to what the speaker is saying.

You should **consider** what the speaker's **body language** is telling you.

Focus on the speaker.

Do:
- take note of the speaker's body language
- take part in one discussion at a time

Don't:
- be distracted or let your mind wander
- start another discussion with someone else in the group

Step 2:
Show the speaker that you are listening

You should make it **clear** to the speaker that you are listening.

Use your **body language** to show you are paying attention.

Do:
- maintain eye contact with the speaker
- use body language that is 'open'

Step 3:
Provide feedback to the speaker

You should make it **clear** to the speaker that you **understand** what is being said.

Show that you **understand.**

Do:
- confirm that you understand by saying, "What I understand from this is that...." "It sounds to me that you are saying that..."
- ask questions if you're not sure what is being said

Step 4:
Wait to comment or contribute

You should **wait** for the **appropriate time** to respond.

Wait your turn.

Do:
- wait patiently
- allow the speaker to finish making his point

Don't:
- interrupt

Step 5:
Respond at the right time and in a way that is suitable to the situation

You should make **appropriate comments** when the speaker has finished making his point

Give an **appropriate response** to the speaker.
Do:
- treat the speaker with respect
- make your point in a tactful way

Don't:
- verbally attack the speaker
- put the speaker down in any way

4

→ Topic, purpose and context

When listening to other people, you should be aware of the *topic* of the discussion, the *purpose* of the discussion and keep in mind the *context* of the discussion.

The topic of the discussion is the subject matter: what you are talking about.

The purpose of the discussion is the reason why you are having the discussion. Not all discussions have an identified purpose. Sometimes we just sit and chat with our friends to 'catch up'. Sometimes, particularly in work situations, we attend meetings or have discussions with colleagues about aspects of our work.

The context of the discussion is the situation in which the discussion is taking place. The context can be an *informal* chat with a group of friends on your way to college or a *formal* meeting with your manager. The context may also be *familiar* to you, which means that you already know most or all of the people involved in the discussion. Alternatively, the context may be *unfamiliar* to you. This means that you are unlikely to know most or even any of the people in the discussion or that the environment is new to you.

The different skills that you use will depend on the purpose and context of the situation. Think about when you listen to your friends. Do you play on your computer or do your nails at the same time as chatting with friends and would you do the same to your manager?

Example 1:
You have noticed the advertisement shown here in the local newspaper and want to find out more information.

- - - - - - - - - - - - →

The advertisement states that you should phone Paul Wilkinson, Head of Administration, for an informal chat if you are interested in the job.

Although it is an informal chat, the context is unfamiliar as you have not spoken with Paul Wilkinson before.

You should use formal language with correct grammar, without using slang words or colloquialisms.

In situations where you are applying for a job or course, make sure that you have prepared beforehand.

Admin Support Clerk

Excellent primary school needs an enthusiastic admin support clerk.

I am looking for a bright and hard-working person to join our admin team at this excellent primary school.

You will be required to work in the busy office, as well as support teachers with admin tasks.

If you are keen and passionate about working for a caring and dedicated team that supports children from our local community, I want to hear from you!

Please phone me on 06543 1287 for an informal chat about the position and for an application pack.

Thank you for your interest,
Paul Wilkinson
Head of Administration

You should:

Begin with a greeting	Hello
State your name and purpose	... My name is Peter Clarke. I am phoning about the job advert in the local newspaper for an admin support clerk. I'd like to find out more information, please.
Allow the other person to reply	Thank you for your call, Peter. The work involves filing, answering the telephone and dealing with queries from the children and their parents or carers. The work is general office duties.
Be very polite	Thank you. The work sounds interesting. I am interested in working in schools. Can you send me an application pack please?
	Of course, Peter. What is your address?
Speak clearly	My address is 21A Long Road, New Town, County New. My postcode is AB23 6PF
	Thank you. The application pack will be posted today.
	Thank you very much for your time. Goodbye.

Top Tip:

Practise interview calls with a friend

When taking part in a telephone conversation, particularly if it is a formal one, try to ensure that you are comfortable, have pen and paper to hand in case you need to note something down and that there is nothing to distract you. It is also a good idea to be in a sitting position as this helps you to keep calm and not feel rushed.

As in a face to face situation, you need to listen carefully to ensure you understand what you are being told or asked.

When making requests or asking questions in unfamiliar contexts you are likely to feel less relaxed and, perhaps, a little nervous. It is likely that you would feel more confident if you plan ahead.

Think about:
- what the other person might want out of the discussion
- what you want out of the discussion.

You could also prepare some suitable questions, about hours of work or future prospects perhaps.

Once the discussion has started you should ask questions, when you are given the opportunity, to show that:
- you have been listening to the other person
- you are interested in the subject
- you have a sensible contribution to make.

You could also indicate that you would like more information about the subject generally or about a particular point being made.

Your questions should be:
- asked politely
- sensible
- clearly expressed
- in standard English, avoiding slang or **colloquial** words (**jargon**).

Top Tip:

Have a friendly, polite attitude.
Listen carefully. Use standard English.

Example 2:

You were successful in your application to become an admin support clerk and now you also support teachers with different tasks. The school wants to teach children about safety on the internet and you have been asked to join a team at the school to discuss what advice should be given to children. The context of the discussion is informal and familiar.

In an informal **group discussion**, there can be distractions if you are trying to listen to the person speaking. Other members of the group may interrupt and cause you to lose the thread of what the speaker is saying. It can be hard to hear if there is a lot of background noise.

- Position yourself so that you are not at the back or on the edge of a group.
- Remember what different members of the group have said when it comes to your turn to contribute.
- It may be useful to have a note pad to jot things down that you want to respond to later.

Top Tip:

Make extended contributions to the discussion by developing points in detail but be careful not to dominate the discussion.

In an informal **group discussion**, you will know the other people quite well and you will feel comfortable when talking to them. You would use informal language, but you should still speak clearly and think carefully about what you want to say or why you hold a certain opinion about a subject.

When presenting an opinion, you should be careful not to offend the other people in the group. You need to be aware that they may have different views on the subject.

It is very important to remember that people from different cultures (or even different parts of the country) or from different religions may have different beliefs on many subjects. This means choosing your words very carefully.

If possible, prepare beforehand. Know the points that you want to develop in the discussion.

The pace of the discussion will depend on whether there is a chairperson. If there is no chairperson, you will need to contribute to a suitable pace by:

- making relevant contributions at appropriate times
- making your point clearly and at not too great a length, using appropriate language
- responding to the points that others make
- choosing your words carefully if you disagree with a point.

Familiar contexts are more likely to be informal, relaxed occasions, where you will feel comfortable and fairly confident.
Remember, it is still important to show respect to the other members of the group by listening to them carefully, ensuring that your facial expressions and body language show that you are interested and that you are considering their points-of-view.

Asking questions can help to keep a discussion going. You could ask a question to show that:

- you have been listening to other people
- you are interested in the subject
- you want to understand what other group members think
- you need more explanation about a point.

Top Tip:

Judge when it is the right time to ask a question.
Use a friendly tone of voice.
Have a friendly facial expression and use friendly body language.

Your questions should be:

- asked politely
- asked when no-one else is speaking
- sensible
- clearly expressed
- in plain English, avoiding colloquialisms.

Example 3:

You have ideas from the discussion for teaching children about safety on the internet and have been asked to chair a meeting with parents on how children can be safe on the internet while at home.

The discussion will be formal and in an unfamiliar context.

This will be a situation where you may not know the other people well or where the context is formal. You may feel less relaxed and you will need to think very carefully about the tone and content of what you say and the language you use.

In this situation, you would use formal language with correct grammar, without slang and without colloquialisms.

You would need to speak clearly and think very carefully about what you want to inform the other people about or why you hold a certain opinion about a subject.

You should prepare beforehand, making sure that you have a good knowledge of the subject.
If you take on the role of chairperson, you will need to monitor the time, ensuring that one person does not dominate. You should encourage each member to contribute and, when time is running out, bring the discussion to a conclusion.

If all group members cannot agree, you will have to agree to differ! As a member of the group, you would need to:
- anticipate when it is appropriate to make a contribution and be ready to do so without interrupting the current speaker
- ensure that your attitude is respectful and positive
- ensure your body language and facial expressions show a positive attitude
- give thoughtful and informative responses
- use formal and subject appropriate language.

Top Tip:

Speak clearly.
Speak slowly.
Don't mumble.
Don't cover your mouth with your hands.
Think before you speak.

When presenting to a group:
- bring any visual aids, props or handouts that will illustrate your talk and support your points
- do not speak too quickly (practise first)
- make sure that all of your audience can hear you
- use notes, but avoid reading word for word
- look at your audience, at least some of the time
- maintain a good pace to hold their attention
- use formal and subject appropriate language
- if appropriate, give out handouts which support your points, usually best at the end or your audience may concentrate on the handout instead of listening to you
- allow people to ask questions - a good idea to try to think what these might be so that you are prepared and feel more confident!

Top Tip:

Be prepared.

→ Respond to questions on a range of topics

Once again, in order to respond to questions, you need to listen very carefully.

What are you being asked for?

Questions can come in many forms, depending on the context and the topic.

In order to respond to questions, you need to listen carefully to what you are being asked.
Questions can come in many forms, depending on the context and the topic.
For example, you may be asked to show that you have understood an explanation or a set of instructions. You may be asked "Do you understand?" to which you could answer simply with yes or no.
On the other hand, you may be asked a question such as, "What do you need to do today at work?" This requires a more detailed answer, although it is still straightforward.

You may be asked for your opinion or to give information about a personal experience. Similarly, you may be asked to explain why you want something, such as a particular job. These questions require a detailed response that is carefully thought through beforehand.

When responding to questions in an informal situation, you would probably only need to give fairly brief answers and you would feel quite relaxed.

When responding to questions in a formal situation, such as a job interview, the interviewer might ask quite searching questions and would expect longer, more thoughtful answers.

What qualities do you have that would make you a good employee?

I am a quick learner; I managed to pass my driving test first time in just six months.
Also, I am very reliable; I was never late for my Saturday job and always did what they asked of me

Top Tip: ⚠

Make sure you listen carefully and answer exactly what you have been asked.
Listen for key words: why, when, how, tell, explain.
Use formal language with correct grammar.
Include technical/subject specific vocabulary when appropriate.

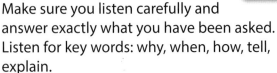

Respect the turn-taking rights of others during discussions

You will need to think about the rights of the other people in the discussion to take their turn and participate equally.

The golden rule is to respect others so that each person feels that they have had an equal opportunity to put their point of view across and that the speaker has been listened to by the rest of the group.

You can help to achieve this by:
- listening carefully to others
- ensuring that your body language is positive
- ensuring that your facial expressions are friendly
- allowing the present speaker to finish what he/she is saying
- trying to make sure that you are not always 'jumping in' first
- signalling (showing by expression or gesture) that you would like to contribute
- ensuring that your tone of voice is polite when you do respond

There are three ways that you can **signal** that you wish to contribute to a discussion:
1. with a change of facial expression, such as a smile
2. with a gesture, such as
   - leaning forward
   - raising your hand
   - a signal agreed by the group beforehand
3. with a phrase, such as
   - Excuse me
   - I'd like to add...
   - Do you think...?
   - That's really interesting...
   - I agree but...
   - I don't agree because...

Top Tip:

Top Tip:
Take turns and signal politely that you want to make a contribution.

➡ Express clearly statements of fact, explanations, instructions, accounts and descriptions

In order to express yourself clearly, you need to:

Consider the purpose and audience 〔1〕
- You may have to inform, explain, instruct or describe.
- Your audience may be a single person or a group of people. The audience may be young children, teenagers or adults. They may know very little or know a lot about the subject.

Consider the context (the setting) 〔2〕
- Tailor your language according to the purpose and audience.
- Tailor your presentation according to whether the context is formal or informal. In a formal situation, you should use formal language with correct grammar, without slang and without colloquialisms. You should speak clearly and choose your words carefully. In an informal situation, you can be more relaxed but should still avoid using slang.

Fully prepare and practise so that you do not forget what you want to say 〔3〕
- It is a good idea to prepare what you want to say beforehand. You could make a note of the main points you want to make to jog your memory as you go along.
- If you have not thought about what you are going to say before you start speaking, you may lose the thread and hesitate or say the wrong thing. Your audience may lose concentration on what you are saying.

Keep concentration 〔4〕
- Pace yourself so that you do not run out of things to say and so that the audience can take in the content but do not get bored.
- It is a good idea to have a glass of water to hand because a drink gives you a moment's pause, stops your throat going dry when talking, and helps concentration and voice projection.

➡ Present information and ideas in a logical sequence

It is important to organise the information and ideas that you want to share, otherwise listeners will find it difficult to understand what you are saying. You need to:

think about the points you want to make

organise the points in a logical order

link these points

support and develop each point with details (examples and/or evidence)

practise your presentation

Top Tip:

Plan and practise

Reading

This section will help you to develop your reading skills and to prepare for the test for Functional Skills in English at Level 1.

To achieve Level 1, you need to do the following:
- Identify the main points and ideas in a text.
- Understand why the author has written a text (the purpose of a text).
- Understand why the author has used particular words (features of the language).
- Understand why the author has presented the text in a certain way (presentational features).
- Use different reading techniques (skimming, scanning and detailed reading).
- Know how to respond to texts.

➡ Understand the purpose of a text

When looking at the different types of texts that we come across every day, it is convenient to think about them according to their purpose.

The *purpose* of a text is the reason why the author decided to write it.
The *audience* of the text is the person or people the author expects to read the text.

The purpose and audience of the text will influence:
- the type of text written
- the language the author uses
- the presentational features of the text.

The language the author uses:
- Style of the language refers to type of language:
  - Formal or informal
  - Objective or subjective

- Tone of the language refers to the tone of voice the author uses:
  - Persuasive
  - Friendly
  - Argumentative
  - Angry
  - Informative
  - Instructive
  - Knowledgeable
  - Balanced
  - Emotive

Later in this section we will look at examples of presentational features and why an author uses them.

Types of texts:
- Letters
- Leaflets
- Books
- Websites
- Instructions
- Emails
- Posters
- Diaries
- Newsletters
- Invitations
- Directions
- Text messages
- Reviews
- Reports
- Newspapers
- Magazines
- Recipes

Presentational features:
- Headings
- Sub-headings
- Paragraphs
- Columns
- Bullet points
- Images
- Photographs
- Logos
- Maps
- Range of fonts
- Bold print
- Use of colour
- Slogans
- Symbols
- Sidebars

In this section, we will examine the type of language used in a variety of texts and the presentational features associated with different types of texts.

To identify the purpose of a text, you should ask yourself, "Why did the author write this text?" There are four common purposes of writing.

Top Tip:

In your assessment, don't just list the features of the text. Say how these features help the author to convey the particular message or idea.

Is the author telling you to do or not to do something or is the author telling you how to do something?

Yes → The author is writing to **instruct** or **advise** you.

No

Is the author telling you information or facts about something?

Yes → The author is writing to **inform** you.

No

Is the author trying to influence you?

Yes → The author is writing to **persuade** you to do something, to buy something or even to believe something.

No

Is the author sharing something with you, such as their beliefs, thoughts and feelings or a story?

Yes → The author is writing to **describe** or **explore** thoughts, feelings, opinions or events or to **entertain** you.

Functional Skills **ENGLISH**

Example: Instructive text

This article is written to **instruct** the reader how to make shortbread.

The type of text is a **page from a book or magazine**.

The audience is anyone interested in cooking.

Features of the language:
- The style of the language is *formal*.
- There is no extra or unnecessary information in the body of the text.
- The language used is easy to read with some *technical* words (stir, beat, roll out) that the reader would need to know.
- The tone of the language is helpful and instructive.
- The author has used *imperative* form of verbs (doing words) to show that instructions are being given.

Shortbread

Preparation time	20 minutes
Cooking time	30 minutes
Makes	25 biscuits

Ingredients

125g / 4oz	Butter
55g / 2oz	Castor Sugar
180g / 6oz	Plain Flour

Preparation Method
1. Heat the oven to 190°C / 375°F / Gas mark 5
2. Beat the butter and sugar together until smooth
3. Stir in the flour
4. Turn onto work surface and roll out gently until 1cm thick
5. Cut into fingers
6. Place on baking tray, pierce with fork and sprinkle with icing sugar
7. Bake in the oven for approx 30 minutes, until golden brown
8. Allow to cool on a wire rack before eating

The presentational features include:
- A *heading*, or *title*. From the title alone, "Shortbread", it would not be clear that the author is giving instructions to bake shortbread using your knowledge of the context of the text – that the recipe is one of many recipes on a website, in a book or magazine dedicated to food – you can work out that the title means, "How to bake shortbread" and not a text about shortbread.
- A *symbol* next to the heading to show that this recipe is suitable for vegetarians without having to write the words.
- *Sub-headings* that are used to organise the information and make the recipe easy to read.
- A *photograph* to make the text attractive, to show the reader what the shortbread looks like and to help the reader to 'picture' what is being cooked.
- Numbered *bullet points* to make the instructions easy to follow and to show that the instructions should be followed in order.

Key Point:

The *imperative* form of a verb (doing word) is the *bossy* form of the verb.
This is where the verb (doing word) is used at the beginning of a sentence, without a subject. Other examples include:

Shut the door!   Don't run!   Stop shouting!   Be quiet!   Eat your dinner now!

Example: Instructive text

This article is written to **instruct** the reader to follow important safety rules at the swimming pool.
The type of text is a **poster** on a wall at a public swimming pool.
The **audience** is members of the public who are using the public swimming pool.

Features of the language:
- The *style* of the language is *formal* and *direct*.
- The *tone* of the language is *instructive*.
- The author has used *imperative* verbs (doing words) to show that instructions are being given.

The presentational features include:
- A *heading*, or title, in **bold print** and in *capital letters* so it is clear from the title what the poster is about.
- The *use of colour* is highly effective: each "don't" is highlighted in red to make reading easy and manageable for all readers.
- *Sub-headings* that are used to organise the information and make it easy to read.
- *Images* to support the instruction that helps you to understand what the instruction means.

POOL RULES

DON'T! RUN

DON'T! DIVE

DON'T! SHOUT

DON'T! PUSH

DON'T! DUCK

DON'T! BOMB

DON'T! PRACTISE ACROBATICS OR GYMNASTICS

Please obey these IMPORTANT rules for your safety and respect other pool users

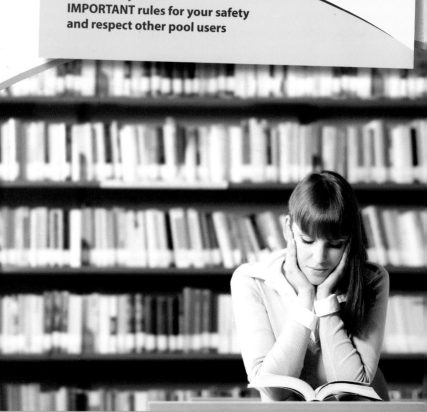

Presentational features

Feature	Examples of why the presentational feature is used
Headings A heading is a title at the head of a text or page of a book.	• Attract your attention to the text • Make the subject of the text clear and obvious
Sub-headings Sub-headings are headings that support the heading and usually follow the heading.	• Make reading more manageable • Highlight important points • Organise information
Paragraphs Paragraphs are sections of a text that deal with different main points.	• Make reading more manageable • Organise information • Highlight important points
Bullet points A 'bullet' is a symbol that is used to show an item, or point, in a list. A bullet point contains information about a main point or idea in the text. It can be a single word, a single phrase or sentence, or a paragraph.	• Make important points clear to the reader • Make reading more manageable • Organise information The symbol used for each bullet can be important. A tick (✔) is used to show that the point is true.
Colours A text can be in either black and white or in colour.	• Make the text stand out • Attract the attention of the reader • Add interest • Make text attractive / interesting
Fonts A font is the style of text used. Common examples include: **arial black** century gothic comic sans verdana **impact** harrington calibri papyrus batang **rockwell** **STENCIL**	A range of font styles is used • to make the text more attractive • to separate different bits of information • to make the text easier to read. A range of font colours is used • to make the text more attractive • to separate different bits of information • to make the text easier to read. A range of font strengths is used • to attract your attention to certain words • to help you to remember what you have read • to make the text easier to read. A range of font sizes is used • to make important points clear to the reader.
Images, photographs and symbols An image is a picture in the likeness of something or someone.	• Illustrate the points made in the text • Make the subject of the text clear and obvious • Explain the text • Add interest

Logos

A logo is a graphic image or an emblem that promotes instant public recognition of an organisation, a company or an individual.

Example: Newsletter

Here is the front page of a newsletter distributed by Sussex Police.

The main purpose of this article is to give tips to aid people living in the area to avoid becoming victims of crime at Christmas.

The type of text is a **newsletter** from Sussex Police to the residents of Crawley.

Newsletters are documents that communicate news and specific information relevant to the target audience. For example, clubs distribute newsletters to members to keep them informed of club activities and charities distribute newsletters to donors to inform them of how their funds have been put to good use.

The contents of newsletters should be factual, accurate and impartial.

The audience of this newsletter is adults living in the area of Crawley.

- Make the text more believable or trustworthy
- Attract the attention of the reader
- Add interest

Pound Hill - December 2011/January 2012

Mistletoe and crime

While gathering your shopping this year, take some time to consider those who may be looking to steal a better deal this Christmas.

It's an unfortunate fact that for some Christmas provides a number of opportunities for criminals to benefit from the good will of others. Sussex Police would like to offer a few tips to help you remain vigilant and reduce the chances of being affected by Christmas and New Year crime:

- Ensure doors and windows are locked at all times and remember to use your alarm if you have one.
- Keys, money and phones are a burglar's dream. Keep all such items well out of sight and reach of doors, windows and letterboxes. Intruders use rods to reach bags and keys and use them to enter your home with ease. In one third of burglaries, the thief didn't have to force entry into the home.
- If you like to display your Christmas tree in your window remember to keep the presents away from prying eyes. Just like anyone else, thieves like to window shop before obtaining their goods.
- Make your home look occupied by using timer switches on your lights and radios so people think you are in. If you don't have them, ask your neighbours to keep an eye on your home and draw your curtains if you are away.
- Dispose of packaging carefully. Empty boxes awaiting collection and bins full of packaging are a perfect advert for burglars.
- Be wary of anyone offering you high price goods at a cut down price. Your bargain could be someone else's Christmas present and handling stolen goods could carry a prison sentence.

© Sussex Police

Crawley

Features of the language:

- The *title* is a play on words: instead of Mistletoe and Wine, the author has chosen to call the article Mistletoe and Crime.
  The title helps to focus the reader's attention on an important subject, while giving the context of the text.
- The *style* of the language is *formal* and *direct*.
- The *tone* of the language is helpful and *instructive*.
- The author has used *imperative* verbs to show that instructions are being given.

The presentational features include:

- A *heading*, or *title*, of the article to attract the attention of the reader and create a link between Christmas and crime.
- The use of short *paragraphs* to organise the information and explain the reason for the article.
- A *bullet point* for each tip. Like the poster, there is no sequence as one action does not follow another, but all the tips are useful. The author of the text gives a reason for each tip to show how the mind of a criminal works.

Functional Skills **ENGLISH**

Example: Instructive text

Here is another example of an instructive text. This is a website that gives directions from one location to another, in this case from Doncaster Railway Station to Highfield's Academy House.

The main purpose of this website is to **instruct** the reader how to get from (A) Doncaster Railway Station to (B) Academy House.

The type of text is a **website** that shows maps and gives directions from one location to another.

The **audience** is members of the public who use the internet to get directions from one place to another place.

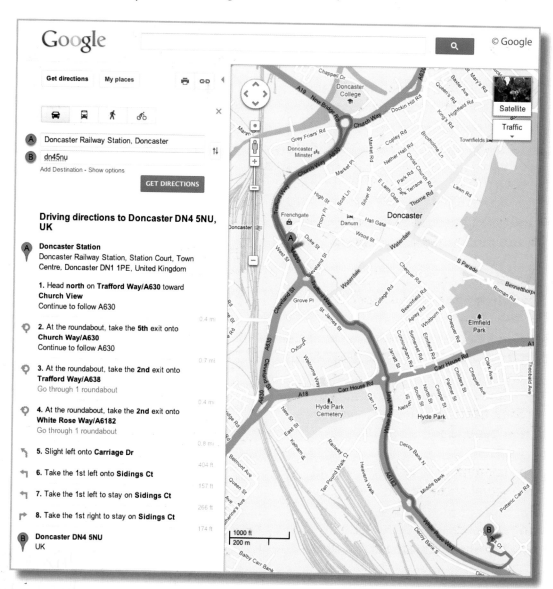

The presentational features include

- a *heading* or title at the top of the list of directions that clearly says exactly what the directions are for
- *numbered bullet points* to show that the directions should be followed in order
- *symbols* for (A) and (B) on the map and next to the written directions to show the start and end of the journey
- *symbols* to the left of each written instruction to give the reader a visual representation of the instruction and aid understanding
- a *map* to show the route
- a range of *font* strength to emphasise main parts of the journey
- the use of colour in the written directions to highlight any difficulties on the route.

Features of the language:

- The *style* of the language is *formal* and *direct*. There is no extra or unnecessary information in the body of the text.
- The *tone* of the language is helpful and *instructive*.
- The author has used *imperative* form of verbs (doing words) to show that instructions are being given.

Instructions can be simple, such as the notice on the tree saying, "Do Not Feed Me," and a line drawing of a squirrel to show who the instruction is from.

Or they can be more complex, such as the instructions that come with a piece of furniture that has to be assembled at home. These instructions can be several pages long and have diagrams to support the written instructions.

Summary:

Language associated with instructive texts:

- The imperative form of a verb is used to show instructions are being given.
- Instructions are clear and direct so that you can understand them without being confused.

Presentational features associated with instructive texts:

- Instructions are listed using bullet points.
- Numbered lists are used if you should follow the instructions in order.
- Key points are sometimes in bold text.
- Colour is used to draw your attention to important points.
- Images are used to help understanding.

Example: Informative text.

The main purpose of the text below is to **inform** the reader about the conservation work that is being carried out at the Zoo. The type of text is a **website** that gives information about the Zoo. The audience is general members of the public, visitors to the Zoo and people interested in conservation at the Zoo.

Key Point:

Articles written to **inform** are clearly written and stick to facts. They answer questions such as who, what, where and when.

Features of the language:
- The style of the language is **formal** and **direct**. There is no extra or unnecessary information in the body of the text. The author of the article does not say what he thinks about conservation at the Zoo and so is not expressing an opinion, nor is he making a suggestion that the reader should visit the Zoo and so is not trying to influence the reader in any way. The text is written purely to inform.
- The tone of the language is **informative** and **factual**.

Conservation at Colchester Zoo

Breeding Programmes

Native Breeding

Conservation Talks

Research at Colchester Zoo

Fundraise for AFTW

Help Us - Donate Today

JustGiving Text Donations

Volunteering On Umphafa

Volunteer at Colchester Zoo

Nature Area Development

The Green Zoo

Mobile and Ink Recycling

Water Conservation

The modern day zoo has many roles to carry out, including conservation, education, animal welfare, research and recreation. Conservation is the principle role of all zoos, as they work to preserve animal species, many of which are endangered. Two of the main ways that Colchester Zoo is involved with conservation are via captive breeding programmes and supporting conservation projects in the wild.

Colchester Zoo is part of a wider network working to conserve species. Here in the UK, we are part of the British and Irish Association of Zoos and Aquaria (BIAZA) and across Europe we are part of the European Association of Zoos and Aquaria (EAZA). EAZA manage the captive breeding programmes on this European level. These programmes involve the monitoring and management of species between different zoos, helping to maintain genetic diversity. This management is highly important for those species at risk of extinction, as the programmes provide 'back up' populations, which could be used for reintroduction projects into the wild or potentially the donation of sperm or eggs to wild populations.

Colchester Zoo also supports conservation in the wild, actively supporting a number of different conservation projects around the world, which are all working to protect endangered species. Colchester Zoo supports these many projects through its charity Action for the Wild, which was set up in 1993 and achieved charitable status in 2004.

The presentational features include:

- a *heading*, or title, that states clearly what the article is about
- the *use of colour* in the title to attract attention and make the article visually attractive
- a *photograph* to show what the article is about and to make the article visually attractive
- the use of short *paragraphs* to organise the information into key points.

Example: Informative text.

The purpose of this wedding invitation is to **inform** the recipients that they are invited to the wedding of Matthew and Danni.

The type of text is an **invitation** that informs the recipients of the details of the wedding.

The audience of an invitation is the particular people to whom the invitation is addressed.

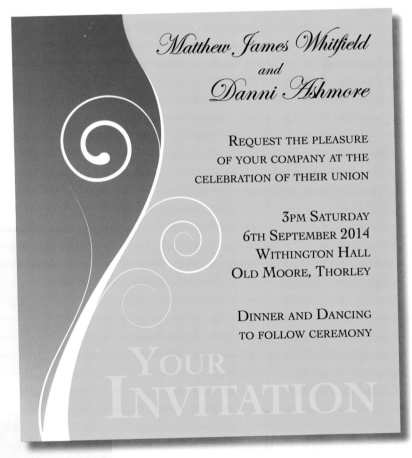

Matthew James Whitfield

and

Danni Ashmore

REQUEST THE PLEASURE
OF YOUR COMPANY AT THE
CELEBRATION OF THEIR UNION

3PM SATURDAY
6TH SEPTEMBER 2014
WITHINGTON HALL
OLD MOORE, THORLEY

DINNER AND DANCING
TO FOLLOW CEREMONY

YOUR
INVITATION

Features of the language:

- The language is *formal*.
- The information is *factual*: who is getting married, when and where and that you, the recipient, are invited.
- The tone of the language is *informative*.

The presentational features include:

- The names of the happy couple presented as a *heading* to attract the attention of the reader and to identify exactly who is getting married.
- Information presented in *paragraphs* or *sections* to show who is getting married, where and when they are getting married.
- A range of *font styles*, *sizes* and *strengths* to attract your attention to important points and to make the invitation look visually attractive.

Top Tip:

Formal texts use a wider range of words. If you don't understand a word, you can use the context of the text to help.

Example: Informative text.

This is a formal letter. The main purpose of this letter is to **inform** the reader that she has been successful in her application for a job and that she is being offered a job.

The type of text is a **formal letter** that gives information about the job.
The audience is a particular woman who applied for a job and was successful in her application.

Employment
Services

Employment Services Ltd
Mayflour House
32-38 Mayflour House
London Road
Leeds
L12 5DT

Tel: 01234 567898
Fax: 01234 567899

Rebecca Jones
34 Leeds Road
Leeds
L34 4SE

12th January 2012

Dear Ms. Jones

Further to your recent interview, I am please to offer you the post of Administrative Assistant with Employment Services Ltd.

I would like to confirm that the hours of work are 9:00 a.m. to 1:00 p.m., Monday to Thursday, which is a 16 hour week. The rate of pay is £7.50 per hour.

Please confirm your acceptance of this position and advise me of your earliest possible start date by 5:00 p.m. on 19th January.

I look forward to hearing from you.

Yours sincerely.

Deborah Perry
Recruitment Manager

Features of the language:
*   The *style* of the language is *formal* and *direct*.
*   The *tone* of the language is friendly and informative.

Key Point:

Formal letters are always polite, even if they are letters of complaint.

The presentational features of a formal letter:

- The **address and telephone numbers of the author** (but not the author's name) are displayed in the top right hand corner. (It is also common for these details to be centralised in the header in electronic documents).

- The **recipient's name and address** are displayed on the left, below the author's contact information.

- The **date of the letter** follows below the recipient's name and address. The position and format of the date are flexible. It can go on either the left or the right and can be written either: 12 January 2012, 12th January 2012 or 12/01/2012

- The **salutation or greeting** is displayed on the left below the date and is always, "Dear..."

If the author of the letter does not know the name of the recipient, then traditionally, "Dear Sir," is written. Nowadays, it is more common to write "Dear Sir/Madam" or, "Dear Sir or Madam" to address both genders.

If the author knows the name of the recipient, then it is polite to use the recipient's title and last name, e.g. "Dear Mr. Rogers" or "Dear Mrs. Appleton."

- The **body of the letter** follows the salutation. It is as short as possible and organised into *paragraphs*. The body of the letter contains the right amount of detail to achieve the author's purpose.
  For example, the letter above informs the recipient that she has been offered a job and informs her of the terms and conditions of that job.
  A letter of complaint would contain sufficient detail in the body of the text to justify a complaint, including relevant fact to support an argument.

- The **close** following the body of the letter is linked to the salutation:

  - If the author knows the name of the recipient, then, "Yours sincerely," is used.

  - If the author does not know the name of the recipient, then, "Yours faithfully," is used.

- The **author's signature** is displayed along with the name of the author.

Key Point:

An abbreviation is a short way of writing a word:
- Dr. is an abbreviation of Doctor.
- Mr. is an abbreviation of Mister.
- Mrs. is an abbreviation of Missus.

Abbreviations start with a capital letter because they are considered to be part of someone's name.

Example: Informative text.

The image to the right shows a text message received by a customer from a supermarket.
It is a message sent to inform the customer that the order will be delivered at a certain time.

The purpose of this text is to inform the customer that the order has been received and when the order will be delivered.

The type of text is a *text message*.

The audience is the customer who placed the order.
It is a generic text, which means that it is the same text that is sent to every customer who has placed an order online to inform them of their delivery time.

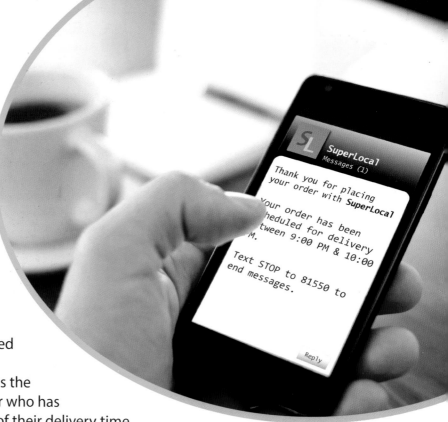

SuperLocal
Messages (1)

Thank you for placing your order with **SuperLocal**

Your order has been scheduled for delivery between 9:00 PM & 10:00 PM.

Text STOP to 81550 to end messages.

Reply

Features of the language:
- The *tone* of the language is *polite*.
- The information is *factual*: when the order will be delivered.

The presentational features include:
- A *heading*, or title, states who the text is from.

Summary:
Language associated with informative texts:
- It is objective: the author is expressing facts without revealing personal opinions or feelings.
- It is formal.
- Technical language that is linked to the subject is sometimes used.

Key Point:

The audience of a text message can be a single person or many people.

Example: Persuasive text.

The purpose of this text is to persuade the reader to become involved in the prevention of animal suffering. The main point of the text is written inside the leaflet - that it is wrong to mass-produce, kill and eat animals.

The type of text is a *leaflet*. The cover of the leaflet is to the right and an extract from the inside is shown below.

The audience is the general public.

Features of the language:
- The tone of the language is *emotive*.

Key Point:

Emotive language is language that is charged with emotion or language that is used to deliberately arouse an emotional response from the reader.

You can help stop the suffering

www.animalaid.org.uk

ANIMAL AID

The presentational features of the cover include:
- A *heading* that attracts your attention by using 'You can...' and by having the word 'suffering' in a larger font and in colour.
- A *logo* that shows who has produced the leaflet and to show the information is trustworthy.
- A *photograph* to show what the leaflet is about and to draw your attention to the leaflet.

Animal Aid has filmed undercover in farms throughout the UK

Some farms were randomly chosen. Others were visited because they operated to 'high welfare' standards or they were run by industry leaders. This is what we found:

- At seven pig farms owned or run by directors of the industry's marketing board, we filmed pregnant and nursing sows **incarcerated in narrow metal crates;** dead, sick and dying piglets littering the pens; and animals wading through filth or living in utterly barren environments.

- Freedom Food is the RSPCA's farm assurance and labelling scheme, under which animals are said to be provided with 'a stimulating environment that enables [them] to exhibit their natural behaviour'. However, at a Somerset Freedom Food farm, we found a large number of **lame, starving, dead and dying broiler chickens** inside a vast windowless unit that held 30,000 birds.

You can see the footage at www.animalaid.org.uk/go/farmingvideos

- At a Dorset goat farm, **a mother lay dead on the shed floor** with a bullet in her head. Her newborn kid huddled beside her body. A second shot goat lay alongside the pair. The farm, whose milk and cheese were sold by leading supermarkets, kept all the goats confined all year round – a system known as 'zero grazing'.

- Zero grazing is increasingly common on larger dairy farms. At four such operations, we filmed cows crowded together in the gloom, with evidence of emaciation and disease. At one farm, **two cows and a young calf had been shot and dumped outside.**

- At a Devon farm rearing turkeys for the Christmas market, we filmed inside a barn holding hundreds of birds. Many were covered in muck, and were **feather-pecked and suffered from deformed feet and legs.** Some were so ill that they couldn't raise themselves from the filthy floor. On top of the feed bins lay long-dead birds.

Sheep face different hardships...

In November 2009, the farming trade press reported that hundreds, if not thousands, of sheep perished in the floods that battered Cumbria. Later came news that a million Scottish sheep faced being starved or frozen to death on exposed hillsides.

These are examples of why a growing number of people believe that it is wrong to mass-produce, kill and eat animals.

The presentational features of the inside include:
- a *range of font colours*, *strengths* and *styles* throughout the text to attract your attention to important points, to make the text visually interesting and to make the text easy for skimming and scanning for information
- a range of *background colours* to organise the text into different sections and make the article easy for the reader to skim read or scan for information
- a *heading*, in a bold font, that clearly states what the article is about
- *bullet points* organise the examples of cruelty into *paragraphs* and make the information manageable to read
- *bold font strengths within the paragraphs* attract the attention of the reader directly to the upsetting acts of cruelty
- a separate *paragraph* about sheep, including a photograph, to bring additional information to the attention of the reader. This is achieved through different *background colour* and *different font colour*, *size and strength*.

(Please note that there were additional photographs and captions that were not included in this extract).

Example: Persuasive text.

Here is a front page of a leaflet about giving up smoking, available from Ulster Cancer Foundation.

The *purpose* of this text is to persuade the reader to give up smoking and to offer the reader help to do so.

The audience is any member of the public who smokes cigarettes.

The type of text is a **leaflet** that provides details of a service that offers help to people who want to give up smoking.

Features of the language:
- The language is *persuasive* and directly engages with you, the reader. Note the use of YOU and YOUR throughout.
- The *tone* of the language is polite.
- The information is *factual*.

The presentational features include
- a *heading*, or *title*, that speaks directly to the reader as 'YOU' to attract your attention
- a *range of font sizes and colours* to highlight individual words and phrases to attract your attention, with 'YOU' written in red to emphasise that this leaflet is aimed at you
- the *use of colour* throughout to make the leaflet visually attractive
- a *photograph* of a dirty ashtray to illustrate what the leaflet is about and to convey the unhealthy nature of smoking.

© Ulster Cancer Foundation

Summary:
Language associated with persuasive texts:
- It is subjective: the author's own opinions and feelings are expressed.
- It can be formal or informal. If it is informal, it is because the author is trying to engage you and bring you on side.
- It often includes emotive language.

Example: Descriptive text.

This text is an example of a ***review*** of a restaurant. There are various websites that collect reviews of restaurants from customers, as well as of holidays, hotels and tourist attractions.

The ***purpose*** of a review is for customers to ***describe*** their experiences: note the high number of adjectives and adverbs used in this example.

The author is not attempting to persuade other readers to go to the restaurant; he is simply describing his experience.
Of course, other readers will be influenced by this review but, remember, we are looking at the main purpose of the text and that is to describe his experience.

Reviewed
13th January 2012

Bird's Nest Restaurant
The Bird's Nest Restaurant, in our opinion, offers unfussy but cleverly thought out dishes. We visited for a 50th birthday treat and were not disappointed. The atmosphere, cleanliness and attention to detail were spot on.

We were blown away by the crab ravioli. It was perfectly cooked and totally delicious. The sauce was creamy and absolutely fanstic, and suited the crab to great effect.

The cheese board was to die for!

One downside - the price! The 4-course meal for four people cost a hefty £655. Not something we can afford regularly but an excellent one off.

Was this review helpful? YES / NO

Summary:
Language associated with descriptive texts:
- It uses adjectives to describe nouns.
- It uses adverbs to describe verbs.
- It can be formal or informal.

 Identify the main points and ideas of a text

At Level 1, you are expected to be able to identify the main points and ideas of a text, which means that you will be able to say, in your own words, what the author of the text is telling you.

To identify the main points and ideas of a text, pick out key words and phrases. Use the headings, sub-headings and any images to help you.
- What are the main points and ideas?
- How are they presented?
- Why have they been included?

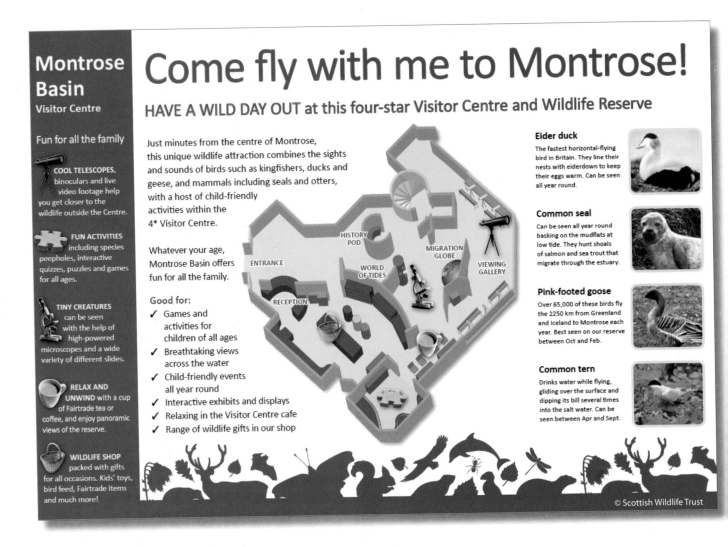

Montrose Basin
Visitor Centre

Fun for all the family

COOL TELESCOPES, binoculars and live video footage help you get closer to the wildlife outside the Centre.

FUN ACTIVITIES including species peepholes, interactive quizzes, puzzles and games for all ages.

TINY CREATURES can be seen with the help of high-powered microscopes and a wide variety of different slides.

RELAX AND UNWIND with a cup of Fairtrade tea or coffee, and enjoy panoramic views of the reserve.

WILDLIFE SHOP packed with gifts for all occasions. Kids' toys, bird feed, Fairtrade items and much more!

Come fly with me to Montrose!

HAVE A WILD DAY OUT at this four-star Visitor Centre and Wildlife Reserve

Just minutes from the centre of Montrose, this unique wildlife attraction combines the sights and sounds of birds such as kingfishers, ducks and geese, and mammals including seals and otters, with a host of child-friendly activities within the 4* Visitor Centre.

Whatever your age, Montrose Basin offers fun for all the family.

Good for:

✓ Games and activities for children of all ages
✓ Breathtaking views across the water
✓ Child-friendly events all year round
✓ Interactive exhibits and displays
✓ Relaxing in the Visitor Centre cafe
✓ Range of wildlife gifts in our shop

HISTORY POD
MIGRATION GLOBE
ENTRANCE
WORLD OF TIDES
VIEWING GALLERY
RECEPTION

Eider duck
The fastest horizontal-flying bird in Britain. They line their nests with eiderdown to keep their eggs warm. Can be seen all year round.

Common seal
Can be seen all year round basking on the mudflats at low tide. They hunt shoals of salmon and sea trout that migrate through the estuary.

Pink-footed goose
Over 65,000 of these birds fly the 2250 km from Greenland and Iceland to Montrose each year. Best seen on our reserve between Oct and Feb.

Common tern
Drinks water while flying, gliding over the surface and dipping its bill several times into the salt water. Can be seen between Apr and Sept.

© Scottish Wildlife Trust

Here is the inside section of a **leaflet** from Montrose Basin Visitor Centre and Wildlife Reserve. The cover of the leaflet is also shown (on the next page) to give context, but the main discussion will focus on the inside section, shown above.

The **purpose** of the leaflet is to attract visitors to Montrose Basin Visitor Centre and Wildlife Reserve.

The **heading** is an invitation to Montrose. Who is the invitation from? Consider the context. The front cover of the leaflet shows the same **heading** as the inside, along with a picture of a bird and the **logo** of the Scottish Wildlife Trust. The main point of the **heading** is to show that you are invited to come to Montrose Basin Visitor Centre by the bird on the front cover, who is also a visitor to the Centre.

Why has the author written the **heading** as an invitation from a bird? To show that Montrose Basin is the reserve that the birds choose and that you should come too.

The **heading** is written in a larger **font size** and in **colour** to attract the attention of the reader and to make the leaflet attractive.
The words in the **heading** are easy to read and understand, showing that the **audience** is the general public.

The **heading** is written as an instruction. Did you notice the **imperative** verb? Did you notice the exclamation mark at the end of the sentence to give a sense of excitement, too?

Key Point:

Use your knowledge and previous experience to work out the overall sense or purpose of a text.

Functional Skills **ENGLISH**

The *sub-heading* includes two very important points about Montrose Basin Visitor Centre and Wildlife Reserve:

- You can "have a wild day out" – this is written as an instruction and in capital letters to attract your attention and to emphasise what an exciting day out you can have at the centre. Did you notice the play on words? Wild refers to the animals at the centre and the excitement you can experience.
- The Visitor Centre has 4 stars, meaning that the Centre offers a high quality experience to the visitors.

The remaining information is organised into *paragraphs*, which makes the text easy to read.

- The first *paragraph* offers key information that is new to the reader. The main points in this *paragraphs* are that the Centre is minutes from the centre of Montrose, unique and child-friendly, and that visitors can see birds and mammals at the Centre. The fact that the Centre has four stars is repeated.
- The following *paragraph* is only one short sentence, stating that the Centre is fun for all the family.
- The list of *bullet points* shows the good things about the Centre. The *symbol* of the tick is used to emphasise that these points are true.

The *image* in the centre of the text shows a map of the different areas of Montrose Basin Visitor Centre and Wildlife Reserve. The *symbols* on the map are explained in the *sidebar* to the left. The *photographs* of the wildlife show what species of mammals and birds can be seen at the Montrose Basin and the *title* or caption of each photograph is in bold text to draw your attention.

The *sidebar* to the left contains extra information.
The *font* is in white on a green background.
The *symbols* used relate to the symbols used on the map.

Come fly with me to Montrose!

Scottish Wildlife Trust

Montrose Basin
Visitor Centre

© Scottish Wildlife Trust

Reading techniques: skimming, scanning and reading for detail

It is not always necessary to read a text word for word.
Skimming and *scanning* are techniques that help the reader to find and obtain information quickly, without reading every word. Skimming and scanning techniques help you to read more quickly.

Key Point:

Skimming is used for getting the general idea of a text.

Key Point:

Scanning is used to locate certain information.

Key Point:

Detailed reading is used to help understanding and involves careful reading of a text

Skimming is used to get a gist of what the author is writing. The gist of an article is the general idea of what the article is about. We skim read to get the general idea before we decide if we want to read the article in full or in detail.

How to skim read a text:
1. Read the title and subtitles to get an idea of what the text is about.
2. Look at the pictures or photographs to get more information about the text.
3. Read the first few sentences.
4. If the article is of interest, read the text by letting your eyes skim over the words and paying particular attention to the parts that are of interest.

Scanning is used to locate specific information within a text. For example, you may wish to look up the start time of a television programme or search for a plumber in the small ads section of a local newspaper.

How to scan a text:
1. Don't read every word. Look over the page to locate words of interest.
2. Use titles, headings and sub-headings to help locate the information.
3. Search the text for the particular word or phrase.

The example text on the following page is taken from a free, local newspaper. The section is written to inform the reader about some of the different activities available in the local area.

The author sticks to facts – date, activity, cost, time, location and a contact telephone number.

The information is clearly organised using headings and dates.

Functional Skills **ENGLISH**

To look for a line dancing class on Tuesday evening, you would:
- Scan the text to locate the section on Dancing.
  There is no need to read the first three sections; in fact, you could ignore them completely.
- Scan the text to locate the subtitle, Tuesday January 24, ignoring the information for the other dates.
- Scan the titles of each entry to identify line dancing classes, ignoring all the detail of each entry.
- Skim read the three entries for line dancing on Tuesday, January 24 to see if any of these classes are of interest to you, for example, at the suitable location and time.
- Read the entry for detail to find out the exact location and who to contact.

Make a Date

Talks & meetings

Friday, January 20
AN EVENING WITH JULIA DICKSON AND JOHN JOHNSON, £10 a ticket, 8pm, South Benfleet Social Club, 18 Vicarage Road, Benfleet. 0128 12345

Wednesday, January 25
EVENING OF MEDIUMSHIP, £5, 7.45pm, The Royal Gatehouse, 21 High Street, Shoebury. 0172 13456

Quiz nights, Games

Saturday, January 21
QUIZ NIGHT, £4, 7.45pm, St Peter's Church Hall, Long Road, Canvey. 0777 12654

Sunday, January 22
POKER NIGHT, £5 per person subject to regulations, 8pm, The Rubber Duck Inn, 24-34 High Street, Benfleet. 0168 12643

Monday, January 23
PUB QUIZ NIGHT, £1 per person, 9pm, The Rubber Duck Inn, 24-34 High Street, Benfleet. 0168 12643
FRIENDS OF THE FORUM QUIZ NIGHT, £10 for table up to 6, 7pm, Thomdon Road Baptist Church Hall, Thomdon Road, Southend. 0172 65421

Tuesday, January 24
THE FOREX ROOM QUIZ NIGHT, Free, 8pm, The Forex Room, Westcliff. 0172 12464

Walks

Saturday, January 21
SOUTH EAST ESSEX RAMBLERS, 8.30am, Moreton via Matching Tye. Bring own refreshments. Phone leader first, 10-12 miles. Meet John Burrows car park, Hadleigh. 0172 12365

Sunday, January 22
SOUTH EAST ESSEX RAMBLERS, 10am, Walkthrough woods to Hadleigh Castle. Return via Thames Drive. 5.5 mile walk. Meet at CP by Balfiars Woods Stables, Leigh. 0172 12465

Wednesday, January 25
SOUTH EAST ESSEX RAMBLERS, 9am, Coggleshall - Lamberts Farm - Swan Street - Gt. Tey. Pub lunch stop. 10 miles. Meet Rawreth Lane car park. 0128 12365
SOUTH EAST ESSEX RAMBLERS, 10am, Five-mile walk. Meet Southend Leisure Centre car park, Garon Park, Eastern Avenue, Southend. 0172 13465

Dancing

Friday, January 20
POLE DANCING LESSONS, £5 per hour, 10am, Pole Fanatics, 319 Canterbury Road, Southend. 0175 69854

Saturday, January 21
DANCE CLASSES - ALL AGES, £4.50-£7.50, 7pm, The Stables Community Centre, Straight Road, Benfleet, 0128 65433
MAJORETTE CLASSES, £3, 9.30am, Eastwood Community Centre, Western Approaches, Southend. 0143 25611
POLE DANCING LESSONS, £5 per hour, 10am, Pole Fanatics, 319 Canterbury Road, Southend. 0175 69854

Sunday, January 22
POLE DANCING LESSONS, £5 per hour, 10am, Pole Fanatics, 319 Canterbury Road, Southend. 0175 69854

Monday, January 23
DANCE JUNKIE SALSA LESSONS, £6, 8.30pm, St Christopher's Hall, London Road, Leigh 0159 89644

Tuesday, January 24
DANCE CLASSES - ALL AGES, £4.50-£7.50, 7pm, The Stables Community Centre, Straight Road, Benfleet, 0128 65433
POLE DANCING LESSONS, £5 per hour, 10am, Pole Fanatics, 319 Canterbury Road, Southend. 0175 69854
STARMODERN LINE DANCE CLUB - ABSOLUTE BEGINNERS TO ADVANCED, £6.50 Adults, 7pm, The Stables Community Centre, Straight Road, Benfleet, 0128 65433
LINE DANCE, 11am, Our Lady of Lourdes Church, Long Road, Rayleigh, 0168 23548
LINE DANCE, 7.30pm, St David's Church, Elm Road, Rayleigh, 0128 13954
ELMSGATE HORTICULTURAL SOCIETY CLUB NIGHT, £1 members, £2 non-members, St Margaret's Church Hall, Elmsgate Drive, Rayleigh.

Wednesday, January 25
CANVEY SALSA CLASSES, £5, 10am, Canvey Ladies Society, London Street, Canvey, 01298 653117
DANCE FUSION - WOMEN'S DANCE & FITNESS CLASS , £5, 7.30PM, St Christopher's Hall, London Road, Leigh 0159 89644
FITNESS CLASS, £5, 7.30pm, Dance City, London Road, Leigh. 0172 323541
SALSA HEART, £7, 8.15pm, Dance City, London Road, Leigh. 0145 12688
POLE DANCING LESSONS, £5 per hour, 10am, Pole Fanatics, 319 Canterbury Road, Southend. 0175 69854
ZUMBA FITNESS, £5, 8pm, Thomdon Road Baptist Church Hall, Thomdon Road, Southend. 0172 65991
BALLROOM & LATIN LESSONS, £3, 2.45pm, St. Anne's Church Hall, Lemon Road, Leigh. 0172 22211

The *textual* and *presentational features* of newspapers and magazines are well-suited to *skimming* and *scanning* techniques, whether they are paper-based or electronic. By *skim reading*, the reader can browse through the newspaper to identify stories or advertisements that are of interest. By *scanning*, the reader can locate articles on a particular topic. The reader would then read the article *in detail*.

Presentational features of a newspaper or magazine article:
- A *headline* that captures the reader's attention. It is short and in bold text.
- An *orientation sentence* that offers an introduction to the article and summarises what the article will be about. This sentence is usually short and maintains hold of the reader's attention.
- A headline or orientation sentence that asks you a question aims to engage you fully.
- The *main body* of text is clearly organised into paragraphs and uses appropriate language for the intended audience.
- A *photograph* or an *image* that offers a snapshot of what the article is about.
- A *caption*, or *title*, of the photograph or image.

➡️ ## Understanding formal and informal language

So far, we have mentioned whether texts discussed were formal, or informal but we have not discussed the features of formal and informal texts.

Formal *language...*	**Informal** *language...*

...is often used in

- public notices
- business letters
- newsletters where the audience is members of the public
- instructional texts, such as directions or rules
- invitations to formal events
- timetables

...is often used in

- persuasive texts, such as adverts
- reviews
- online discussions with friends using social media
- text messages to friends

...uses a wide range of vocabulary

"Simon cannot attend the meeting."
"I might apply for the position I saw advertised in the local newspaper."
"Please give this matter your urgent attention."

...uses a limited range of vocabulary

"Simon can't go to the meeting."
"I might go for the job I saw in the paper."
"You'd better get this sorted, asap."

Contractions are not used in formal language

"We are unable to go."
"Peter has no credit on his phone" or
"Peter does not have credit on his phone."

Contractions are used in informal language

"We can't go."
"Peter hasn't got any credit on his phone."

➡ Reading information contained in tables and charts

Below is an extract from a train timetable. Timetables are organised in columns to make them easy to read. The first train leaves Shoeburyness at 05:35 and arrives at London Fenchurch Street at 06:42.

Note the blank spaces or lines on the timetable. They show that the train does not stop at this station on this journey.

The train that leaves Shoeburyness at 06:11 does not stop at Basildon, Laindon or West Horndon.

Also note that timetables are liable to be amended regularly and that you should always check for up-to-date versions.

Example: You are travelling from Chalkwell to Barking. You have agreed to meet your friend at 10:00 at Barking Station. What time do you need to catch the train at Chalkwell Station?

Scan the timetable for the information that you need. It is not necessary to read the whole document.

1. **Locate** Chalkwell and Barking in the list of stations on the left hand side.
2. **Locate** the time of the train that arrives at Barking before 10:00. The last train before 10:00 is at 09:55.
3. **Read up the column** from 09:55 to the time that train arrives at Chalkwell. The train arrives at Chalkwell at 09:18.

SUNDAYS

Shoeburyness	0535	0605	0611	0635	0705	0711	0735	0805		0835		0905		and	2035		2105	
Thorpe Bay	0538	0608	0614	0638	0708	0714	0738	0808		0838		0908			2038		2108	
Southend East	0541	0611	0617	0641	0711	0717	0741	0811		0841		0911		at	2041		2111	
Southend Central	0544	0614	0620	0644	0714	0720	0744	0814	0820	0844	0850	0914	0920		2044	2050	2114	2120
Westcliff	0546	0616	0623	0646	0716	0723	0746	0816	0823	0846	0853	0916	0923	the	2046	2053	2116	2123
Chalkwell	0548	0618	0625	0648	0718	0725	0748	0818	0825	0848	0855	0918	0925		2048	2055	2118	2125
Leigh-on-Sea	0551	0621	0628	0651	0721	0728	0751	0821	0828	0851	0858	0921	0928	same	2051	2058	2121	2128
Benfleet	0555	0625	0632	0655	0725	0732	0755	0825	0832	0855	0902	0925	0932		2055	2102	2125	2132
Pitsea	0559	0629	0636	0659	0729	0736	0759	0829	0836	0859	0906	0929	0936	mins	2059	2106	2129	2136
Basildon	0602	0632		0702	0732		0802	0832		0902		0932			2102		2132	
Laindon	0605	0635		0705	0735		0805	0835		0905		0935		past	2105		2135	
West Horndon	0610	0640		0710	0740		0810	0840		0910		0940			2110		2140	
Upminster ⊖	0616	0646	0709	0716	0746	0809	0816	0846	0909	0916	0939	0946	1009	each	2116	2139	2146	2209
Barking ⊖	0625	0655	0717	0725	0755	0817	0825	0855	0917	0925	0947	0955	1017		2125	2147	2155	2217
West Ham ⊖ DLR	0631	0701	0723	0731	0801	0823	0831	0901	0923	0931	0953	1001	1023	hour	2131	2153	2201	2223
Limehouse DLR	0636	0706	0728	0736	0806	0828	0836	0906	0928	0936	0958	1006	1028		2136	2158	2206	2228
London Fenchurch Street DLR ⊖	0642	0712	0734	0742	0812	0834	0842	0912	0934	0942	1004	1012	1034	until	2142	2204	2212	2234

© Train Planning Department, c2c Rail

You will need to catch the 09:18 train from Chalkwell to meet your friend at 10:00.

Top Tip:

Remember that you do not want to be late for your friend, so the train that arrives after 10:00 would be too late.

→ Identifying suitable responses to texts

At Level 1, you are expected to identify suitable responses to texts. This means that you should know what the author expects you to do when you have read the text.

You might have to follow instructions to complete a task. For example, the author of the job advert that we looked at earlier in the book asks you to phone for an informal chat.

Admin Support Clerk

Excellent primary school needs an enthusiastic admin support clerk.

I am looking for a bright and hand-working person to join our admin team at this excellent primary school.

You will be required to work in the busy office, as well as support teachers with admin tasks.

If you are keen and passionate about working for a caring and dedicated team that supports children from our local community, I want to hear from you!

Please phone me on 06543 1287 for an informal chat about the position and for an application pack.

Thank you for your interest,
Paul Wilkinson
Head of Administration

HALF PRICE MOT △△
£27.42

Redeem in branch or book at
www.highfieldauto.co.uk
enter code HF280 at checkout

Consider the text to the left.
This is an advertisement in a local newspaper that offers 50% off the cost of an MOT on your car. An MOT is a test that any car that is over three years must pass every year to prove that it is roadworthy.

This advertisement is aimed at car owners who need to have an MOT on their cars.

If you were interested in responding to this text, you would follow the instructions given: "Redeem in branch".

This means that you would need to cut out the coupon, as shown by the symbol of the scissors, and take the coupon into the branch where you will get your MOT done.

Top Tip: ⚠

Read a text carefully for instructions on how to respond.

Functional Skills **ENGLISH**

Writing

This section is about writing.
To achieve Level 1, you need to do the following:
- write clearly and include appropriate detail (clear and coherent)
- consider the context (the setting)
- consider the purpose (why you are writing)
- think about your audience (who you are writing for)
- plan and draft your writing
- organise your writing into paragraphs or sections so that your reader can understand what you want to say (structure into logical sequence)
- use words and sentences to help the reader understand what you want to say (use of language)
- set out your writing to help your reader understand what you want to say (format and structure)
- spell words correctly
- use sentences and punctuation to make what you are saying clear to the reader (correct grammar and punctuation)
- make sure that your reader can understand your handwriting or word-processing
- check and correct your writing

 ## Writing a range of texts

We will be looking at many different texts that you might need to know how to write.
With each one, we will look at the different things that we must consider when planning and writing:

- Purpose
- Context
- Audience
- Length and detail
- Logical sequence
- Use of language
- Format and structure

 ## A formal letter of complaint

Purpose	to inform your audience about your dissatisfaction
Context	you have returned from a disappointing shopping trip
Audience	the manager of the shop
Length and detail	to support your complaint you should develop details in paragraphs
Logical sequence	• introductory paragraph signalling your dissatisfaction • one paragraph for each area of disappointment • conclude with summarising sentence and what you would like to be done

Planning – this simple flow chart may help you to plan:

1 Introduction saying what you have bought and why you are disappointed with the item

2 Poor service when you went to the shop

3 What was wrong with the item when you got it home

4 Unhelpfulness of staff when you took the item back

5 Concluding paragraph asking for refund and improvement for the future

Use of language – you should use formal language:

Use correct grammar and punctuation.

Use technical or specialist words, if appropriate.

Use formal language:

- Don't use text language, e.g. gr8 (great).
- Don't use slang or colloquial expressions, e.g. hard cheddar (misfortune).
- Don't use abbreviations or contractions, e.g. I wasn't happy (I was not happy).

Format and structure – it should look like a formal letter with:

- your address in the top right hand corner
- recipient's address
- date
- dear Sir or Madam
- introductory paragraph on new line
- paragraphs 2, 3 and 4 each on a new line
- concluding paragraph on a new line
- close, e.g. 'Yours faithfully' or 'Yours sincerely'
- signature
- name printed.

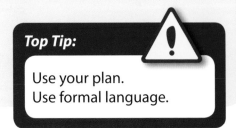

Top Tip:

Use your plan.
Use formal language.

Example letter

2 Farway Road
Anytown
XX1 2YY

01.08.11

The Manager
Youthstore
Anytown
XX1 2ZZ

Dear Sir

I am writing to you to complain about the trousers that I bought from your store last week. They are of poor quality and do not fit me properly.

Your members of staff were rude and unhelpful when I arrived. They kept me waiting for a long time and served other customers who arrived after me. They could not find the colour that I wanted and did not apologise for this. There was a queue for the fitting room and I had to leave to catch my bus. I decided to buy the trousers and take them home to try them on.

When I tried the trousers on at home, they did not fit well. The material felt rough and uncomfortable and the colour did not go with my other clothes. I decided to take the trousers back to your store.

When I asked for my money back, the assistant refused, saying that I should have tried them on in the shop. He told me that they were sold at a reduced price so could not be taken back.

I am very upset as I had used my birthday money to buy the trousers and I needed a new pair. I would like my money back and a letter of apology. I think you should take steps to make sure that your members of staff explain things carefully and politely to customers in the future.

Yours faithfully,

Sam Humphrey

Sam Humphrey

Functional Skills **ENGLISH**

An informal email:

Purpose	to persuade
Context	there is an opportunity to volunteer at an old people's home in your town
Audience	a college/school friend
Length and detail	brief description of the opportunity, reasons why you both should do this
Logical sequence	• introduction describing the opportunity • middle paragraph setting out three reasons for doing this • final sentence to persuade

Planning – this is a short, informal task.
Write brief notes, perhaps as below; also jot down some useful words:

- The opportunity

- Reasons _____

  _____

  _____

- Final sentence (persuading)

- Emotive and descriptive words, e.g. exciting, fun, helpful, impressive, different

Use of language – your language should be informal (chattier than in a formal letter) and you should be:
- definite
- positive
- persuasive
- personal

You should also include questions and you should repeat yourself for emphasis.

Format and structure – it should look like an email with:
- your email address, date and time
- friend's email address
- subject
- Dear ....
- introductory sentence/paragraph on a new line
- middle paragraph with reasons on a new line
- final, persuasive sentence on a new line
- sign off (informal e.g. See you soon)
- your name

Example email

From,   Jobloggs7@example.com
To,   Patsmith190@example.co.uk
Subject, This sounds great, read this!
Date,   Friday, 10 June 16.45

Hi Pat

Remember Mr Jones said we should be doing something to help people in our town? I've just seen this advert asking for young people to help out at the old people's home. It looks just the job for us, not too far away and lots of variety so we won't get bored.

Just look at all the different things we could do. They want help in the gardens – a good chance to build up our muscles and stamina for football! They need help serving meals. Wouldn't that be good practice for your work experience in the restaurant? They're asking for people to chat/play games with the old people which sounds dead easy. They also want people to run errands which could mean an interesting trip to the shops. We can go at times to suit us so we'd still be able to play football and on our xboxes! If we do this it would impress our future employers and we might even enjoy meeting new people!

I'd really like to do this with you as we could have a laugh and help each other out if things get embarrassing or difficult. Also, I reckon it'd be great for our CVs. Please, please give it a go!

Hope to hear from you soon.

Jo

Purpose	to tell/instruct someone to do something
Context	write a recipe for a student cookbook
Audience	other students
Length and detail	• make each step/instruction brief and clear • include a detailed list of ingredients
Logical sequence	• name of recipe • list of ingredients • list of instructions in order that the cook needs to them • finish with cooking or serving advice

Key Point:

The **imperative** form of a verb (doing word) is the **bossy** form of the verb.
This is where the verb (doing word) is used at the beginning of a sentence, without a subject.
Other examples include:
Shut the door!   Don't run!   Stop shouting!   Be quiet!   Eat your dinner now!

Planning – you may not need to plan in detail if the recipe/task is simple. Make notes if you need to.

Use of language –
• Use imperative verbs.
• Use simple words that everyone can understand.
• Use short, simple sentences.
• Include specialist words (e.g. 'beat mixture strongly').
• Use punctuation.

Format and structure – make it look like a recipe with,
• name of recipe
• subheading and list of ingredients
• subheading – Method – and list of steps/instructions
• cooking/serving advice

*Note –these instructions must be followed in the right order. Instructions for a different process
e.g. for a computer game, a science experiment or how to use a washing machine might look slightly different.*

Example recipe

Peanut Butter Cookies

Ingredients
125g peanut butter (crunchy or smooth)
125g honey
200g plain flour
Pinch of salt
A little milk

You will need:
Mixing bowl
Measuring scales and spoon
Rolling pin
Baking sheet

Method
1. Mix together peanut butter and honey
2. Mix in flour and salt to make a stiff dough
3. Add a little milk if dough is crumbly
4. Roll out to 10mm thick
5. Bake on greased baking sheet at 180 degrees for 12 minutes

When cool cut into squares.

 Instructions (non-sequenced)

Purpose	to instruct
Context	your parents have gone away and left you in charge of the house
Audience	you!
Length and detail	brief and clear
Logical sequence	• salutation • brief points • signature

Use of language –
• imperative verbs
• simple words
• informal

Format and structure –
note form (could be stuck on the fridge!)

Hi Sam

Remember!

Lock the doors when you go out

Feed the cat

Clean the bird cage

No wild parties!

A leaflet:

Purpose	to inform
Context	you are starting a new club at school/college
Audience	younger students

Length and detail

you need to write brief details about,
- people involved
- activities
- when
- where
- how to join

You also need to include photos/pictures (but for an assessment do not spend time drawing pictures, just show that you would put a picture in for a real leaflet.)

Logical sequence

you need to have:
- name of club
- who you are
- who it is for
- activities
- when it will happen
- where it will happen
- how to join

Planning – you might like to make a visual plan like this:

Name of club	Activity 1 - describe and picture	Why people should join
Photo of students painting and potting	Activity 2 - describe and picture	When the club will meet
Who is starting the club	Activity 3 - describe and picture	Where it will meet and pictures
Who it's for	Activity 4 - describe and picture	How to join (website address)

Use of language – informal and persuasive. Remember to use punctuation.

Format and structure – include,
- title/name of club
- details of activities
- when and where
- how to join

You could write in columns (as in the plan) or sections one under the other.

Example leaflet

ART club

KEY STAGE 3

YEAR 11 STUDENTS ARE STARTING AN **ART** CLUB FOR YEARS 7 & 8

WOULD YOU LIKE TO HAVE FUN?

WOULD YOU LIKE TO BE CREATIVE?

ACTIVITIES

Sketching
We will learn to draw still life, people, nature (animals, trees, flowers and many other things). We will sometimes go outside to sketch.

Pottery
We will learn to shape clay and use a wheel to make many lovely things – we could even make presents for the family!

Sculpting
We will learn to make paper, wood and metal sculptures. They may be small or really big and impressive!

You will work on your own or in a group, whatever you want. We will help you to be artists. The art teacher has offered to come and help and make sure that we use the equipment safely.

www.artistsattownschool@sch.com

WHY JOIN?

YOU WILL HAVE FUN
YOU WILL LEARN NEW SKILLS
YOU WILL MAKE NEW FRIENDS
YOU WILL BECOME MORE CONFIDENT

The club will meet on Tuesdays after school. You will need to bring an old shirt or overall. You may bring a snack to eat before we start.
We will meet in the Art Studio. If the weather is good we may sometimes go outside to sketch or sculpt.

To join, sign up on our website
www.artistsattownschool@sch.com

HURRY BECAUSE WE HAVE TO LIMIT NUMBERS!

Top Tip:

!

Think about layout.
Make your leaflet clear and attractive.
Use a large font for titles.

A formal report:

Purpose	to inform
Context	• your local leisure centre has asked you to sample new activities for teenagers • the manager has asked you to write a report about your experience
Audience	the manager of the leisure centre
Length and detail	• describe the activities and say what you liked or disliked • develop detail in paragraphs
Logical sequence	• introductory paragraph saying what you were asked to do • one paragraph for each activity and comments (what you liked or disliked) • concluding paragraph summarising your experience

Planning – you may find a simple flow chart helps you to plan,

Introduction saying what you were asked to do

Activity 1 and comments

Activity 2 and comments

Activity 3 and comments

Concluding paragraph summarising what you liked or disliked and a suggestion for improvement

Use of language
– use formal language, correct grammar and punctuation to make your writing clear.

Format and structure – it should look like a report with,
• heading
• introductory paragraph on a new line
• paragraphs 3, 4 and 5 each on a new line
• concluding paragraph
• your name and the date

Functional Skills **ENGLISH**

Example report

New Activities at Newtown Leisure Centre - Report for the Manager

As you requested, I have spent the last week trying out the new activities programme for teenagers. You asked me to write a report saying what I liked and disliked about the activity programme. I made some notes while I was trying out the activities. Here is my report.

On Tuesday, I went to the boxercise class. There were a lot of older boys and girls there which made me worry that they would all be better than me. It was much better than I expected because the instructor was young and made us feel welcome. He told us not to worry if we had not done kickboxing before. He showed us the basic moves and helped us to practise them. Although I was tired by the end of the session, I felt that I had made progress and I certainly had fun. The older boys and girls were kind and did not laugh at my efforts.

On Thursday, I went to multi-aquatics. I can swim though I am not very good and I was unsure what we would be doing. The teacher started with a talk about safety. Then she asked us to swim a length while she made notes on our ability. Next, she divided us into lanes and taught us how to do front crawl. After ten minutes we all did aqua-aerobics which was much more interesting than swimming up and down the pool. In the last ten minutes we played team games. That was good fun and I was tired again!

On Saturday, I went to indoor tennis. I had never played tennis so I was a bit worried. The teacher showed us how to hold a racquet and how to serve the ball. Then we played hitting backwards and forwards in pairs which was really rather boring. The teacher sat there reading a book while we played. I think she should have been helping us to improve our technique.

I think it is a great idea to run classes especially for teenagers. I made a new friend and I felt fitter at the end of the week. I like the boxercise class best because we did different fun things and the teacher made me feel good. The multi-aquatics session was quite good, but I did not enjoy the swimming part as much as the aerobics and games. The indoor tennis was disappointing. It would have been much better if we had received more teaching. I think you could improve the programme by offering a choice of indoor games like basketball and badminton. It would also help if you gave the instructors some more training in teaching teenagers.

I hope you find this report helpful.

Chris Smith   25.07.2012

Top Tip:

Use formal language.
Use correct grammar.
Use correct punctuation.
Use different conjunctions.

Functional Skills **ENGLISH**

→ An informal report:

Purpose	to describe
Context	you have decided to adapt the formal report for your fellow students in the form of an article for the student newsletter
Audience	fellow students
Length and detail	this report will be shorter with main points only
Logical sequence	• introductory paragraph • middle paragraph describing activities • concluding paragraph

Planning – you may only need to write a few notes or possibly highlight main points on your copy of the formal report.

Use of language
– informal and personal.

Format and structure – it should look like an article with:
• a title
• paragraph with main points
• a summary
• a signature

Example informal report

An Opportunity to Get Fit

Hi Guys,

I've just had an interesting week trying out a new activities programme at our local leisure centre. I thought I'd share what I discovered with you.

Tuesday was boxercise class. Although there were a lot of older kids there, the instructor made me feel ok. We did lots of basic moves and it was good fun, but tiring. On Thursday I went to multi aquatics which was good and bad. We did swimming, aqua-aerobics and team games. The team games were cool but the swimming was boring. Saturday was the worst day with indoor tennis. The teacher was useless and sat reading while we just batted the ball around.

Overall, I reckon the idea of special classes for teenagers is good but they need to offer more options and some of the instructors need to get their act together. I've sent a report with suggestions for improvement to the manager so watch this space for more news!

Chris Smith 26.07.12

Top Tip:

Use an informal style.

A proposal:

Purpose	to explain ideas
Context	you are concerned about health and safety at your place of work
Audience	the manager
Length and detail	• state the purpose of your proposal • paragraphs detailing areas of concern • paragraph suggesting improvements • concluding, summarising paragraph
Logical sequence	• introductory paragraph saying what the proposal is about • paragraph detailing concerns • give reasons why the manager should sort out these problems • suggestions for improvements • concluding paragraph summarising and persuading

Planning – you could use a flow chart as before or you could use a spider diagram (as below) to help you think of ideas.

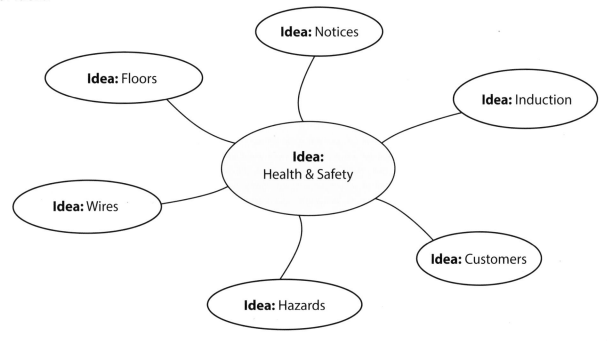

Use of language
– use formal language and include technical/specific words. Use punctuation to make your meaning clear.

Format and structure – it should look like a formal proposal with:
- a title
- introductory paragraph on a new line
- paragraphs 2, 3 and 4 each on a new line
- concluding paragraph on a new line
- your name and date

Functional Skills **ENGLISH**

Safety at Work

I have now been working for Robbins and Company for four weeks and while I have been doing my induction I have seen some health and safety problems. I have noticed these because I did a course on health and safety at college before coming to Robbins and Company.

The first problem that I noticed was the state of the floors in the mornings. Because the cleaners come in early in the morning, the floors are still wet and there are no notices warning the employees. Last week, I slipped over because I was rushing to get in on time. Luckily, I did not injure myself but someone else could have a nasty accident.

The second problem is the electrical wires trailing over the floors and hanging down from the ceilings. People could trip and get caught on these and be injured. This is an even bigger hazard because people could get electric shocks and there could even be an electrical fire.

I hope that you do not mind me writing this but I am really concerned about health and safety and felt I should tell you because I nearly got hurt and somebody else might. Also, if customers came in and had an accident they might sue you! I am sure there must be other hazards and I think you should do a detailed risk assessment of your factory. If you do not, then you could end up in court for not carrying out your duties as a manager. Also, your employees will be much happier and work better if they feel safe and cared for.

I hope that you will take note of my concerns and put matters right.
Ali Khan 25.09.12

→ Reply to invitation:

Purpose	to inform
Context	a neighbour invites you to a street party and asks for ideas for the party
Audience	party organiser (your neighbour)
Length and detail	• brief acceptance • brief explanation of ideas
Logical sequence	• acceptance • ideas for food and drink • ideas for entertainment • sign off

Planning – write brief notes -
- acceptance
- food for adults
- food for children
- drinks for adults
- drinks for children
- entertainment for adults
- entertainment for children
- sign off

Use of language – you should be chatty and informal. Use punctuation to make ideas clear.

Format and structure – it should include:
- acceptance with date, time and place of party
- ideas for food and drink
- ideas for activities
- your name and date of reply

Hi John, thank you for the invitation to New Avenue street party on 5th June 2012 at noon in the avenue.

I would love to come.

I think the children would like to have crisps, savoury snacks, cupcakes and ice cream.

They would like cola and juices to drink.

I think the adults would like sandwiches, pies and crisps.

They would probably like a non-alcoholic punch, especially if they are driving, but could be invited to bring wine or beer if they wished.

The younger children will probably get bored!
I think you should get a clown to entertain them.

Some of the adults might want to watch sport so I think you should have a tv screen for them.

If you want some help, let me know.

Phil Jones (number 6) 1st May 2012.

Top Tip:

Use your notes.

Purpose	to inform and instruct
Context	to provide briefing notes for a new student
Audience	new student
Length and detail	provide short notes to instruct student on aspects of school/college
Logical sequence	• introduce and explain purpose • take student through a day in time order • concluding sentence

Planning – you may find a mind map would help you think of all the things you need to include.

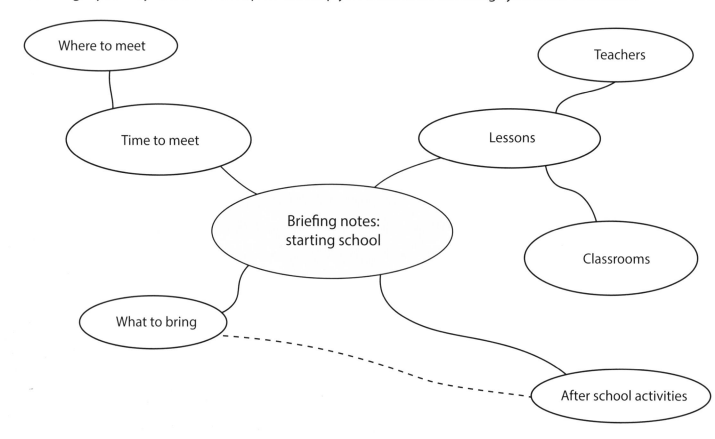

Use of language – you should be chatty but clear. Use punctuation to make your ideas clear.

Format and structure – it should look like briefing notes
• heading
• introductory sentence
• bulleted points
• concluding sentence
• your name and date

Briefing Notes for New Student

These notes should help you on your first day at Newtown High:

- School starts at 9 a.m. but arrive by 8.45 a.m.
- Come to the gate on Park Road, not the main road. I will meet you there.
- Bring a bag with your pens and pencils, science overall and PE kit. It needs to be big enough for books as well.
- Bring a snack for break time or money for the tuck shop.
- Cloakrooms are on the first floor.
- Your tutor base is on the first floor. Turn left at the top of the main staircase.
- Your tutor is Mr. Somali. He will tell you about assembly and give you your timetable.
- Lessons start at 9.15. You have science first double.
- Morning break is at 10.45. I will meet you at the football field and show you the grounds.
- Lunch is at 12.30. You will need money or a packed lunch. The canteen food is ok!
- Afternoon lessons start at 1.30 and finish at 3.30. You start with PE.
- Your tutor will give you a list of after school activities.
- I go to 5 a side football. You could join me!
- Activities finish at 4.30.
- You need to leave by the same gate as in the morning. Don't forget your homework!

Good luck with your first day. Call me on my mobile (07555 7012345) if you want to chat before the day.

Ali Smith 30.08.12

Planning – Sometimes you do not have to plan the sequence of your writing or think about the format because it is done for you. You are most likely to meet these forms and formats when you go into the workplace. Here are some examples that you might meet and be asked to complete. You will still need to think carefully about what you write.

An application form

7. Any other information you would like to include

Application for **Employment**

Vacancy applied for _____

Personal details:

1. Title _____
   First name _____
   Surname _____

2. Address (including postcode) _____
   _____
   _____
   _____

3. Daytime telephone number _____
   Evening telephone number _____

4. Email address _____

5. Work experience (starting with the most recent first)

Employer	Job and dates of work	Reason for leaving

6. Education

School/college attended	Qualifications gained or course attended

Reference 2	
Names	
Address	
Telephone number	
Email address	
Occupation	

...he information I have given is correct. (Print and sign)

_____
_____
_____

Notes:
- When you fill in a form, follow the instructions carefully; for example you should list your employment experience starting with the latest job.
- Always be truthful!
- Include any information that would be useful for the job – for example, if applying to work in a children's nursery, baby-sitting experience would be useful, but the employer would not be interested in where you went on holiday.
- It is useful to keep a copy of the application in case the employer telephones you or invites you for interview.
- Remember that it is polite to ask your referees if you may give their names.

An accident report form

Top Tip:

Remember to read forms carefully and fill them in accurately.

Accident Report Form

| Person's name | Age | How did the accident occur? |

| Date | Time | |

| Anyone else present | |

| Place of accident | |

| Equipment involved | First aid given |

| Part of body involved | Treatment by whom |

| Description of injury | Further action taken |

| Signature | |

A timesheet

Newtown Biscuits Employee Timesheet

Employee Name _____

Hours worked	a.m.	p.m.
Monday		
Tuesday		
Wednesday		
Thursday		
Friday		
Saturday		
Sunday		

Signature _____ Date _____

Notes –
- You will need to keep a record of your hours so that you can fill in the form.
- Complete all cells.
- If you do not work on a particular time period, e.g. Saturday p.m., enter 0.

Grammar, Style and Punctuation

We have looked in detail at planning, structure and format of writing. We thought about the most suitable language to make our ideas clear for the audience and purpose of the writing.
Using correct grammar, punctuation, style and spelling also help to make writing clear for the reader.

Here are the basic rules you must follow:

→ **Write in proper sentences.**

→ **Make sure subjects and verbs agree.**

→ **Use the correct tense throughout your writing.**

→ **Use the correct style of writing.**

→ **Join your sentences with a wide range of conjunctions.**

→ **Don't let your sentences run on and on. Punctuate them!**

→ **Spell correctly!**

 ## Proper sentences

- Every sentence must make sense. It is a complete thought.
- Every sentence must have a verb (a doing or being word).
- Every sentence must have a subject (the word that goes with the verb e.g. The boy ran).

Examples:

'Down the road'
...does not make sense on its own.

'The boy down the road'
...still does not make sense. It has a subject (the boy) but no verb.

'The boy ran down the road'
...does make sense now that we have added the verb (ran).

Single subjects
are followed by singular verbs.

Example: The girl **is** playing.

Plural subjects
are followed by plural verbs.

Example: The children **are** playing.

Remember, when the **subject** consists of **two or more nouns** joined by the word '**and**' the verb is plural.

Example: 'Tom and Ali' **are** playing.

People often make mistakes with the following words. Don't make the same mistake. These words have a singular verb:

Each	Somebody	Every	Everyone	Anyone
Nobody	Everybody	One	No-one	Someone

A ***collective noun***
also has a singular verb.

Example: The class was told to go home.
The school is in the town.

People sometimes make mistakes matching verbs with pronouns (e.g. 'You was late.'; 'He don't listen.'; 'It were cold.'). Note that we are talking about ***Standard English*** that we should use when writing. In some parts of the UK the local spoken dialect may use these 'incorrect' forms in normal conversation.

Pronouns are words which take the place of nouns.
These are the different pronouns:

First person: I, we (the person speaking).
Second person: you (the person spoken to).
Third person: he, she, it, they (someone or something else).

The table below shows you which verb goes with which pronoun.

Pronouns	He / She / It	I	We / You / They
	is	am	are
Verbs	was	was	were
	does	do	do
	has	have	have

As a general rule, you should ***keep to the same tense throughout a writing text***. For example: a story is usually written in the past tense (although speech between characters may be in the present tense). Look back at some of the text types in the first part of this section:

- The formal letter of complaint – the first and last paragraphs are about the writer's feelings at the time of writing and are in the present tense, but the rest of the letter is in the past tense because it is describing what happened.
- The informal email – is mainly in the present tense as the writer is saying what he/she wants now
- Instructions (as in the recipe) – are written in the present tense.
- The leaflet and the proposal – are written mainly in the future tense as they are saying what you could do in the future.
- The report – is written in the past tense as it is describing the writer's experience.

 Style

Use words and phrases that suit the purpose and the audience. They should sound right.
Look back again at some of the text types in the first part of this section:

- The letter of complaint, the proposal and the report are written in formal language and include precise words that fit the text (for example, 'poor quality', 'apologise', 'material', 'reduced price', 'activities', 'aerobics' 'safety', 'volunteers', 'sponsorship'.) These texts do not contain shortened words such as 'don't'.
- The informal email, reply to invitation and briefing notes use informal language such as shortened words and a chatty style (for example, 'Hi Pat' instead of 'Dear Sir/Madam' and 'give it a go').

Joining sentences

When you join sentences, ***use a wider range of conjunctions*** than 'and', 'then', 'so' and 'but'. Sometimes conjunctions like: because, if, who, when, where, while will give you more precise meaning and improve your style. For example:

'We took an umbrella so we would not get wet.'	 *...could be written...*	**'We took an umbrella because we did not want to get wet.'**
'We went to a theme park and had a good time.'	 *...could be written...*	**'We went to a theme park where we had a good time.'**

Punctuation

Don't run your sentences into one long confusing sentence. For example:

'The end of lesson bell sounded the class all rushed to the door Dan suggested they played football.'

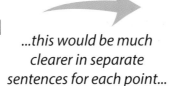 *...this would be much clearer in separate sentences for each point...*

'The end of lesson bell sounded. The class all rushed to the door. Dan suggested they played football.'

***Every statement must begin with a capital letter and end with a full stop**.*
> Example, 'It is cold today.'

) ***The names of people, places, organisations, countries, counties, days of the week and months of the year must also have capital letters**.*
> Example, 'The dog ran away from Ali on Sunday.'

i) ***A question must end with a question mark.***
> Example, 'Is it cold today?'

✓) ***An exclamation must end with an exclamation mark.***
> Example, 'Wow, that was exciting!'

') ***Colons should be used at the beginning of a list.***
> Example: 'For our picnic we took with us: sandwiches, crisps, cakes and drinks.'

If you remember these rules, your writing will be clear.

Spelling

Correct spelling is also important in helping your writing to be clear.
Here are a few ideas to help you with learning and remembering spellings:

i) Train yourself to use a *dictionary* to check your spellings. Jot down words on a post-it, stick them on your bedroom wall and learn them.

ii) Use *mnemonics* (memory helpers). For example, remember that fortun**ate** contains **ate**.

iii) Say the word in your head the way it is spelt. For example, cup-board for cupboard.

iv) Split long words into smaller parts (*syllables*). For example, rest-au-rant for restaurant.

v) Sort words into families. For example: refuse, refused, refusing, refusal.

vi) Learn words in spelling rule groups. For example, the 'magic e' – hop, hope (the e at the end of a word changes the short vowel into a long one).

vii) Write down the word, cover it so you cannot see it, try to remember what it looked like and spell it (write or say the letters), uncover and check. If you got it wrong, do the process again.

viii) Watch out for *homophones* (words that sound the same but are spelt differently).
For example: their (belonging to them; they're (= they are); there (where) and where (place); wear (i.e. your clothes); and here (where); hear (what happens when you listen).

Try to think of a way to remember.
For example: Remember ear is in hear, and the 'place' here is in where and there.

ix) Try to learn the most commonly used words.

At the back of this book there is a list of 1,000 most useful words.
Try to learn 5 that you do not know each day. Another 'five-a-day'!

Spelling Rules

i) *Plurals*
   We add <u>s</u> to make the plural of a word.
   For example,   school   ⟶   schools
                    college   ⟶   colleges

Note the following exceptions:
- We add **es** to words ending in **ss sh ch x**
   For example,   cla<u>ss</u>   ⟶   clas**ses**
                    di<u>sh</u>   ⟶   dish**es**
                    bat<u>ch</u>   ⟶   batch**es**
                    bo<u>x</u>   ⟶   box**es**

- We add **ies** to words ending in **y** if there is a consonant before the y
   For example,   bab<u>y</u>   ⟶   bab**ies**
                    fl<u>y</u>   ⟶   fl**ies**

   If there is a vowel before the **y**, we simply add **s**
   For example,   to<u>y</u>   ⟶   toy**s**

- We change the **f** into **ves** to words ending in **f**
   For example,   thie<u>f</u>   ⟶   thie**ves**

- We add **es** to some words ending in **o**
   For example,   potat<u>o</u>   ⟶   potato**es**

- Some words are exceptions to the rules!
   For example,   child   ⟶   chil<u>dren</u>
                    mouse   ⟶   mice
                    man   ⟶   men
                    woman   ⟶   women
                    sheep   ⟶   sheep

ii) *Doubling the consonant*

Consonants are the letters of the alphabet that are not vowels.
The vowels are *a e i o u*

If the word ends in a CVC pattern (consonant, vowel, consonant),
we double the consonant before adding **ed** or **ing**.

For example,	hug	⟶	hug**ged**
	trap	⟶	trap**ped**
	top	⟶	top**ping**
	fit	⟶	fit**ting**

Note the following exceptions:

- Words ending in **w x y z** do not follow this rule.

- Words ending in **e**, for **ed** just add **d** and for **ing**, drop the **e** and add **ing**.

| For example, | tile | ⟶ | tile**d** |
| | race | ⟶ | raci**ng** |

- Two syllable words
If the stress is on the first syllable when you say the word out loud,
we <u>do not</u> double the consonant before adding **ed** or **ing**

For example,	limit	⟶	limit**ed**
	open	⟶	open**ing**
	wander	⟶	wander**ing**

If the stress is on the second syllable when you say the word out loud,
we <u>do</u> double the consonant before adding **ed** or **ing**

For example,	deter	⟶	deter**red**
	permit	⟶	permit**ted**
	forget	⟶	forget**ting**

iii) *Words ending in y*

If there is a consonant before the **y**, change it to **i** before adding **ed**,
but just add **ing**.

| For example, | carry | ⟶ | carri**ed** |
| | carry | ⟶ | carry**ing** |

If there is a vowel before the **y**, just add **ed** or **ing**.

| For example, | stray | ⟶ | stray**ed** |
| | stray | ⟶ | stray**ing** |

iv) *Suffixes*

Suffixes can be added to the ends of nouns to make them into adjectives.
The spelling of the noun usually stays the same.

For example:

		But sometimes the spelling changes:
fool,	foolish	
child,	childish	For example:
water,	watery	athlete, athletic
fault,	faulty	energy, energetic
music,	musical	sun, sunny
accident,	accidental	permit, permission
comfort,	comfortable	fame, famous
fashion,	fashionable	nature, natural
poison,	poisonous	value, valuable
danger,	dangerous	fury, furious
wretch,	wretched	marvel, marvellous
sense,	senseless	
picture,	picturesque	

v) *Prefixes*

Prefixes are letters added at the start of a word to change its meaning.
They do not change the spelling of the original (root) word.

- **in**, **un**, **im**, **ir**, **mis**, **dis** often form the opposite.
  For example: **in**consolable, **un**known, **im**perfect, **ir**responsible, **mis**judge, **dis**approve.

- **Pre** and **fore** mean 'in front' or 'before'.
  For example: **pre**fix, **fore**ground.

- Other prefixes include **ex**, **re** (meaning again).
  For example: **ex**change, **re**place.

We are coming to the end of the writing section.
There are many other examples of text types, of grammar, punctuation and spelling rules. Some of these will be covered in the accompanying Workbook.

Finally, it is very important that you develop the skills to *review*, *edit* and *check* your writing at each stage.

Remember to *plan* before you begin, *draft* if you have time and, if it is a longer piece of writing, review and edit that draft.
Finally, check that it makes sense, that you punctuated your sentences correctly, that you have used correct grammar and that you have spelt correctly. Then you will be a good writer!

→ Glossary

A

abbreviation	a shortened word e.g. don't = do not
active listening	this is when we concentrate totally on what we are hearing and show this to others
advice	guidance/recommendations/suggestions
anticipate	work out what comes next/expect
appropriate	suitable
assess	to judge performance/ability
audience	who you are writing for/speaking to

B

body language	this is when we use gestures (movements) and facial expressions to show our reactions/feelings e.g. if we turn away we show lack of interest

C

checking	we make sure that spelling, punctuation and grammar are correct
coherent	holds together
collective noun	a noun that stands for a group, e.g. a flock of birds, a college
colloquial	familiar, informal talking/writing
colon	punctuation used before a list e.g. The girl brought: pens, pencils, a ruler and a rubber
communication	the process of passing information
concluding paragraph	the ending paragraph that finishes your writing
conjunction	these are words that join two sentences together or two parts of a sentence together, such as ***and***, ***but***, ***or***, ***nor***, ***for***, ***yet***, ***so***, ***although***, ***because***, ***since***, ***unless*** e.g. the following two sentences can be made into a longer sentence by adding because: "The dog was running. It was chasing a cat." (The dog was running <u>because</u> it was chasing a cat)
consider	think about
consonant	letters that are not vowels
context	the setting
culture	people's beliefs and expected behaviour

D

describe	relate/tell about
descriptive	tells you about something
detail	things you include to show what you are saying

E

editing	when we find an error we edit it out and correct it
emotive	expresses feeling
exception	in spelling, a word that does not follow the spelling rule, e.g. child, children
exclamation	to cry out or to write with strong emphasis e.g. He shouted "Stop!"
explain	to give details about something
eye contact	eyes meeting, showing awareness of another person

F

facial expression	the look you have on your face to show how you feel, such as a smile shows you are happy, a frown shows you are unhappy or that you don't understand something, crying shows you are very sad
fact	something known to be true or correct
formal	official
format	the way your writing is set out

G

grammar	correct use of language
greeting	acknowledge/recognise someone by saying or writing words such as hello/Dear Mr Jones

H

heading	a title
hearing	this is the physical ability to make sense of sounds
homophone	words that sound the same but are spelt differently e.g. their, there, they're

I

imperative verbs	a verb that commands/tells you to do something
inform	to communicate/tell
informal	friendly
ingredients	component parts, e.g. what we put together to make a cake
instruct	to order/teach
introductory paragraph	the beginning paragraph that sets out your purpose

K

key words	words that will alert the reader to a message or theme

L

language	words that we use
layout	how writing is set out on a page
listening	this skill is what we do when we take notice of what we hear
logical sequence	the parts follow each other in a sensible way

M

method	the way you should do something and the order in which you should do it
mnemonic	a way of remembering something e.g. to help remember how to spell fortunate, it contains ate

N

noun	a naming word, e.g. tree

O

opinion	someone's view

P

personal	appertaining/belonging to a person
persuade	to convince somebody to do something
phrase	a group of words that does not have a verb e.g. the long, cold winter
plural	more than one
prefix	a letter or letters added to the beginning of a word to change it e.g. known/unknown
presentational feature	the features used to present a text
process	how you do something
pronoun	pronouns stand for nouns to avoid repetition e.g. The boy ran and **he** caught the dog
purpose	why you are writing/speaking

R

recipient	person who receives something
relevant contribution	add something suitable
respect	to consider other people
responding	reply/answer/react
reviewing	to look back e.g. when we finish a piece of writing we review it to ensure there are no errors or omissions (things left out)

S

salutation	greeting
scan	to locate specific information within a text
signal	show
singular	one person or thing
situation	where something is happening
skim	to read quickly for a gist of the text
specialist words	like technical words
Standard English	written or spoken English that is grammatically correct and contains no colloquialisms
stress	in spelling, this affects whether or not we double the consonant before adding a suffix e.g. if the stress is on the first syllable as in limit we do not double when adding ed but where stress is on second syllable as in permit, we do
structure	the combination of the parts
sub-heading	a title that introduces a new section
subject	in grammar, this is the word that identifies who or what is being or doing something, or what the sentence is about, e.g. **Sam** is swimming. Sam is doing something and is the subject of the sentence The **boy** is playing with the dog. The boy is the subject because he is the one doing something
suffix	a letter or letters added to the end of a word to change it e.g. fool (noun) foolish (adjective)
syllable	a part of a word containing one sound e.g. con-tain-ing has three syllables
symbol	a presentational feature that is used to represent something else

T

tailor	make something fit/appropriate
task	something you have to do
technical words	words that are particular to a subject, e.g. a vehicle = type of transport such as a ca
tense	this shows when something is happening - in the past, present or future
thread	the theme that connects the parts of what you want to say when talking or writing

V

verb	a doing/being word e.g. he swims/she is. Verbs give the time something happens by their tense (see tense)
volunteer	someone who offers to do something (often unpaid)
vowel	a, e, i, o, u all other letters are consonants

W

word family   words with the same root word,

For example,   **refuse** ⟶ refused ⟶ refusal

                    home ⟶ homeless ⟶ homely

Acknowledgements

The authors and publisher would like to thank the following individuals and organisations for permission to reproduce copyright material in the Functional Skills Leve1 Handbook and accompanying Workbook:

Sussex Police

Google maps

Colchester Zoo   www.colchester-zoo.com

Animal Aid

Ulster Cancer Foundation

Scottish Wildlife Trust / Montrose Basin Visitor Centre

The train planning department, c2c: The timetable is for illustration purposes only and should not be mistaken for up-to-date information for travel.

NSCPCC   "10 Ways To Keep Your Child Safe" is taken from the NSPCC's publication "Out alone: Your Guide to Keeping Your Child Safe". This leaflet is available to download from www.nspcc.org.uk/parenting or can be ordered by calling 0808 800 5000 or emailing help@nspcc.org.uk. More information and advice leaflets for parents and carers can also be found at www.nspcc.org.uk/parenting.

If you are worried about a child, need advice or want to talk, the NSPCC is here to help, 24 hours a day, seven days a week, free of charge.   Call 0808 800 5000, text 88858 or email help@nspcc.org.uk.

Norfolk Wildlife Trust

1,000 most useful words

ABLE	ATTACK	CASE	DAY	EMPLOY
ABOUT	ATTEMPT	CASTLE	DEAD	END
ABOVE	AVERAGE	CATCH	DEAL	ENEMY
ACCEPT	AWAY	CAUSE	DEAR	ENGLISH
ACCEPTABLE	BACK	CEMETERY	DECIDE	ENJOY
ACCIDENTALLY	BAD	CENTRE	DECLARE	ENOUGH
ACCOMMODATE	BALL	CERTAIN	DEEP	ENTER
ACCORD	BANK	CHANCE	DEFEAT	EQUAL
ACCOUNT	BAR	CHANGE	DEFINITE	EQUIPMENT
ACCOUNTABLE	BASE	CHANGEABLE	DEGREE	ESCAPE
ACROSS	BATTLE	CHARACTER	DEMAND	EVEN
ACT	BE	CHARGE	DEPARTMENT	EVENING
ACTIVE	BEAR	CHIEF	DEPEND	EVENT
ACTOR	BEAUTY	CHILD	DESCRIBE	EVER
ACTRESS	BECAUSE	CHOOSE	DESERT	EVERY
ACTUAL	BECOME	CHURCH	DESIRE	EXAMPLE
ADD	BED	CIRCLE	DESTROY	EXCEPT
ADDRESS	BEFORE	CITY	DETAIL	EXCHANGE
ADMIT	BEGIN	CLAIM	DETERMINE	EXERCISE
ADOPT	BEHIND	CLASS	DEVELOP	EXIST
ADVANCE	BELIEVE	CLEAR	DIE	EXPECT
ADVANTAGE	BELONG	CLOSE	DIFFERENCE	EXPENSE
ADVENTURE	BELOW	CLOUD	DIFFICULT	EXPERIENCE
AFFAIR	BENEATH	COAL	DIRECT	EXPERIMENT
AFTER	BESIDE	COAST	DISCIPLINE	EXPLAIN
AGAIN	BEST	COIN	DISCOVER	EXPRESS
AGAINST	BETWEEN	COLD	DISTANCE	EXTEND
AGE	BEYOND	COLLEGE	DISTINGUISH	EYE
AGENT	BIG	COLONY	DISTRICT	FACE
AGO	BILL	COLOUR	DIVIDE	FACT
AGREE	BIRD	COLUMN	DO	FACTORY
AIR	BLACK	COME	DOCTOR	FAIL
ALL	BLOOD	COMMAND	DOG	FAIR
ALLOW	BLOW	COMMITTEE	DOLLAR	FAITH
ALMOST	BLUE	COMMON	DOOR	FALL
ALONE	BOARD	COMPANY	DOUBT	FAMILIAR
ALONG	BOAT	COMPLETE	DOWN	FAMILY
ALREADY	BODY	CONCERN	DRAW	FAMOUS
ALSO	BOOK	CONDITION	DREAM	FAR
ALTHOUGH	BOTH	CONSIDER	DRESS	FARM
ALWAYS	BOX	CONTAIN	DRINK	FAST
AMONG	BOY	CONTENT	DRIVE	FATHER
AMOUNT	BRANCH	CONTINUE	DROP	FAVOUR
ANCIENT	BREAD	CONTROL	DRY	FEAR
AND	BREAK	CORN	DUE	FEEL
ANIMAL	BRIDGE	COST	DUTY	FELLOW
ANOTHER	BRIGHT	COTTON	EACH	FEW
ANSWER	BRING	COULD	EAR	FIELD
ANY	BROAD	COUNCIL	EARLY	FIGHT
APPARENT	BROTHER	COUNT	EARTH	FIGURE
APPEAR	BUILD	COUNTRY	EAST	FILL
APPLY	BURN	COURSE	EASY	FIND
APPOINT	BUSINESS	COURT	EAT	FINE
ARISE	BUT	COVER	EFFECT	FINISH
ARM	BUY	CROSS	EFFICIENT	FIRE
ARMY	BY	CROWD	EFFORT	FIRST
AROUND	CALENDAR	CROWN	EGG	FISH
ARRIVE	CALL	CRY	EIGHT	FIT
ART	CAN	CURRENT	EITHER	FIVE
ARTICLE	CAPITAL	CUT	ELECT	FIX
AS	CAPTAIN	DANGER	ELEVEN	FLOOR
ASK	CAR	DARK	ELSE	FLOW
ASSOCIATE	CARE	DATE	EMBARRASS	FLOWER
AT	CARRY	DAUGHTER	EMPIRE	FLY

FOLLOW	HOME	LIBRARY	MORNING	OUGHT
FOOD	HONOUR	LIE	MOST	OUT
FOR	HOPE	LIFE	MOTHER	OVER
FORCE	HORSE	LIFT	MOTOR	OWE
FOREIGN	HOT	LIGHT	MOUNTAIN	OWN
FOREST	HOUR	LIKE	MOUTH	PAGE
FORGET	HOUSE	LIKELY	MOVE	PAINT
FORM	HOW	LIMIT	MRS	PAPER
FORMER	HOWEVER	LINE	MUCH	PART
FORTH	HUMAN	LIP	MUSIC	PARTICULAR
FORTUNE	HUNDRED	LISTEN	MUST	PARTY
FOUR	HUSBAND	LITERATURE	NAME	PASS
FREE	IDEA	LITTLE	NATION	PAST
FRESH	IF	LIVE	NATIVE	PAY
FRIDAY	IGNORANCE	LOCAL	NATURE	PEACE
FRIEND	ILL	LONG	NEAR	PEOPLE
FROM	IMMEDIATE	LOOK	NECESSARY	PER
FRONT	IMPORTANT	LORD	NECESSITY	PERHAPS
FULL	IN	LOSE	NEED	PERMIT
FURNISH	INCH	LOSS	NEIGHBOUR	PERSON
FUTURE	INCLUDE	LOVE	NEITHER	PICTURE
GAIN	INCREASE	LOW	NEVER	PIECE
GAME	INDEED	MACHINE	NEW	PLACE
GARDEN	INDEPENDENT	MAIN	NEWS	PLAIN
GAS	INDUSTRY	MAINTENANCE	NEWSPAPER	PLAN
GATE	INFLUENCE	MAKE	NEXT	PLANT
GATHER	INSTEAD	MAN	NIGHT	PLAY
GENERAL	INTELLIGENCE	MANNER	NINE	PLEASE
GENTLE	INTEREST	MANUFACTURE	NO	POINT
GET	INTO	MANY	NOBLE	POLITICAL
GIFT	INTRODUCE	MARK	NONE	POOR
GIRL	IRON	MARKET	NOR	POPULAR
GIVE	IT	MARRY	NORTH	POPULATION
GLAD	JOIN	MASS	NOT	POSITION
GLASS	JOINT	MASTER	NOTE	POSSESS
GO	JOINTED	MATERIAL	NOTICE	POSSESSION
GOD	JOY	MATTER	NOTICEABLE	POSSIBLE
GOLD	JUDGE	MAYBE	NOW	POST
GOOD	JUST	MEAN	NUMBER	POUND
GRATEFUL	JUSTICE	MEASURE	NUMERICAL	POVERTY
GREAT	KEEP	MEET	NUMEROUS	POWER
GREEN	KILL	MEMBER	OBJECT	PREPARE
GROUND	KIND	MEMORY	OBSERVE	PRESENT
GROUP	KING	MENTION	OCCASION	PRESIDENT
GROW	KNOW	MERE	OCCASIONALLY	PRESS
GUARANTEE	LACK	METAL	OF	PRESSURE
HALF	LADY	MIDDLE	OFF	PRETTY
HAND	LAKE	MIGHT	OFFER	PREVENT
HANG	LAND	MILE	OFFICE	PRICE
HAPPEN	LANGUAGE	MILK	OFFICIAL	PRIVATE
HAPPY	LARGE	MILLION	OFTEN	PRIVILEGE
HARD	LAST	MIND	OH	PROBLEM
HARDLY	LATE	MINER	OIL	PRODUCE
HAVE	LATTER	MINIATURE	OLD	PRODUCT
HE	LAUGH	MINISTER	ON	PROFIT
HEAD	LAUGHTER	MINUTE	ONCE	PROGRESS
HEAR	LAW	MISS	ONE	PROMISE
HEART	LAY	MISSPELL	ONLY	PROOF
HEAT	LEAD	MISTER	OPEN	PROPER
HEAVEN	LEARN	MODERN	OPERATE	PROPERTY
HEAVY	LEAVE	MOMENT	OPINION	PROPOSE
HEIGHT	LEFT	MONDAY	OPPORTUNITY	PROTECT
HELP	LEISURE	MONEY	OR	PROVE
HERE	LENGTH	MONTH	ORDER	PROVIDE
HIGH	LESS	MOON	ORDINARY	PROVISION
HILL	LET	MORAL	ORGANISE	PUBLIC
HISTORY	LETTER	MORE	OTHER	PULL
HOLD	LEVEL	MOREOVER	OTHERWISE	PURPOSE

PUT	SALT	SOME	TELL	VICTORY
QUALITY	SAME	SON	TEMPLE	VIEW
QUANTITY	SATURDAY	SOON	TEN	VILLAGE
QUARTER	SAVE	SORT	TERM	VIRTUE
QUEEN	SAY	SOUL	TEST	VISIT
QUESTION	SCARCE	SOUND	THAN	VOICE
QUESTIONNAIRE	SCENE	SOUTH	THE	VOTE
QUITE	SCHOOL	SPACE	THEN	WAGE
RACE	SCIENCE	SPEAK	THERE	WAIT
RAISE	SEA	SPECIAL	THEREFORE	WALK
RANK	SEASON	SPEED	THEY	WALL
RATE	SEAT	SPEND	THING	WANT
RATHER	SECOND	SPIRIT	THINK	WAR
REACH	SECRET	SPITE	THIRTEEN	WATCH
READ	SECRETARY	SPOT	THIRTY	WATER
READY	SEE	SPREAD	THIS	WAVE
REAL	SEEM	SPRING	THOUGH	WAY
REALISE	SELL	SQUARE	THOUSAND	WE
REALLY	SEND	STAGE	THREE	WEALTH
REASON	SENSE	STAND	THROUGH	WEAR
RECEIPT	SENSITIVE	STANDARD	THROW	WEDNESDAY
RECEIVE	SEPARATE	STAR	THURSDAY	WEEK
RECENT	SERIOUS	START	THUS	WELCOME
RECOGNISE	SERVE	STATE	TILL	WELL
RECOMMEND	SERVICE	STATION	TIME	WEST
RECORD	SET	STAY	TO	WESTERN
RED	SETTLE	STEEL	TODAY	WHAT
REDUCE	SEVEN	STEP	TOGETHER	WHEN
REFERRED	SEVERAL	STILL	TON	WHERE
REFUSE	SHADOW	STOCK	TOO	WHETHER
REGARD	SHAKE	STONE	TOP	WHICH
RELATION	SHALL	STOP	TOTAL	WHILE
RELATIVE	SHAPE	STORE	TOUCH	WHITE
RELEVANT	SHARE	STORY	TOWARD	WHO
RELIGION	SHE	STRANGE	TOWN	WHOLE
REMAIN	SHINE	STREAM	TRADE	WHY
REMARK	SHIP	STREET	TRAIN	WIDE
REMEMBER	SHOOT	STRENGTH	TRAVEL	WIFE
REPLY	SHORE	STRIKE	TREE	WILD
REPORT	SHORT	STRONG	TROUBLE	WILL
REPRESENT	SHOULD	STRUGGLE	TRUE	WIN
REPUBLIC	SHOULDER	STUDENT	TRUST	WIND
RESERVE	SHOW	STUDY	TRY	WINDOW
RESPECT	SIDE	SUBJECT	TUESDAY	WINTER
REST	SIGHT	SUBSTANCE	TURN	WISE
RESTAURANT	SIGN	SUCCEED	TWELFTH	WISH
RESULT	SILENCE	SUCH	TWELVE	WITH
RETURN	SILVER	SUFFER	TWENTY	WITHIN
RHYME	SIMPLE	SUGGEST	TWO	WITHOUT
RHYTHM	SINCE	SUMMER	TYPE	WOMAN
RICH	SING	SUN	UNDER	WONDER
RIDE	SINGLE	SUNDAY	UNDERSTAND	WOOD
RIGHT	SIR	SUPPLY	UNION	WORD
RING	SISTER	SUPPORT	UNITE	WORK
RISE	SIT	SUPPOSE	UNIVERSITY	WORLD
RIVER	SITUATION	SURE	UNLESS	WORTH
ROAD	SIX	SURFACE	UNTIL	WOULD
ROCK	SIZE	SURPRISE	UP	WOUND
ROLL	SKY	SURROUND	UPON	WRITE
ROOM	SLEEP	SWEET	USE	WRONG
ROUGH	SMALL	SWORD	USUAL	YEAR
ROUND	SMILE	SYSTEM	VACUUM	YES
ROYAL	SNOW	TABLE	VALLEY	YESTERDAY
RULE	SO	TAKE	VALUE	YET
RUN	SOCIAL	TALK	VARIETY	YIELD
SAFE	SOCIETY	TAX	VARIOUS	YOU
SAIL	SOFT	TEACH	VERY	YOUNG
SALE	SOLDIER	TEAR	VESSEL	YOUTH

Functional Skills ENGLISH